The Covenant

A Study Guide for Deuteronomy

Rebecca Minelga

ISBN 978-0-9982974-4-6

Liminal Publishing
4407 Tom Marks Rd
Snohomish, WA 98290
www.rminelga.wordpress.com

Scripture quotations taken from the (NASB®) New American Standard Bible®, Copyright © 1960, 1971, 1977, 1995 by The Lockman Foundation. Used by permission. All rights reserved.
www.lockman.org

Cover and Map graphics provided by Shutterfly, used under Standard License.
www.shutterfly.com

For the Women of Hope, who always pushed me to go deeper.

For Beth Moore and Jen Wilkin, who showed me how.

And for you, dear one, the faithful woman pursuing the heart of God.

Table of Contents

Introduction

Why should I study the Old Testament? I hear this question often, and maybe it is one that resonates in your mind today, as you embark on this journey. There are myriad reasons to do so, but I will only name a few here.

First, the Old Testament is the very culture and history of every one of the New Testament writers. We cannot risk forgetting that Matthew, Mark, Luke, and John; Paul, James, and Peter, all were first Jewish in their heritage and their beliefs. Jesus, Himself, was the quintessential Jew, a Jew who completely and perfectly fulfilled every aspect of the Old Testament Law. We simply cannot understand the fullness of New Testament scripture without understanding the richly complex and vibrant context that it grew out of.

Second, if our entire faith pursuit is centered, as it ought to be, on knowing God more, it would be highly irresponsible of us to seek after Him while simultaneously rejecting two-thirds of the scriptures that would allow a more intimate understanding of Him, His nature, and His character. Imagine marrying someone but refusing to understand that person's childhood, their high school and college years, or the life they lived before you arrived on the scene. What an empty, self-serving relationship that would be.

Finally, there is no question that the Old Testament is filled with spiritual instruction and application that is still relevant today. This is why Beth Moore wrote studies on Daniel, Esther, and Psalms. This is why the idea of a "David and Goliath" story permeates our modern culture. This is why Psalm 23 is one of the most beloved, most published, most translated portions of poetry in the world, ever.

The scriptures are God-breathed, *all* of them. Even the parts that make us uncomfortable. Even the parts that we don't fully understand. Even the parts that seem (*choke, gasp*) *boring*. Yep, even the construction instructions of the tabernacle and all those genealogies are divine. As Paul says, "All Scripture is God-breathed and is useful for teaching, rebuking, correcting and training in righteousness." (2 Tim. 3:16, NIV) Not just some. Not just the New Testament, which, incidentally, didn't even exist at the time that Paul was writing to Timothy. When he spoke of "all scripture," he was specifically speaking of the Old Testament, the only scripture available at that time.

With that said, perhaps you may be asking a different question, now. *Why should I study Deuteronomy?* Oh, dear one, the answer to that one is so much easier!

Jon Monson states "From a canonical perspective one might say that 'all roads lead to Deuteronomy' because its theological truths lie at the heart of both the Old Testament and the New."[1] Likewise, Christopher Wright wrote of it,

> "Deuteronomy has aptly been described as the heartbeat of the Old Testament. Feel the pulse of Deuteronomy and you are in touch with the life and rhythm of the whole Hebrew Bible. Indeed, if we add the influence of the book on Jesus, Paul, and the early NT church, it is a profoundly significant book in the whole Christian canon of scripture."[2]

Finally, E. Achtemeier says, "There is no book of more importance in the Old Testament and no Old Testament book more basic for understanding the New Testament than Deuteronomy."[3]

This brings us to our first reason for studying this book: it is the beating heart of Jesus' ministry and of the New Testament. In fact, Jesus quotes Deuteronomy more than any other single Old Testament book – eleven times – and it is cited more than eighty times throughout the remaining books of the Bible. Every legal question posed to Him he answered out of Deuteronomy. After Jesus is challenged by the Pharisees for performing a healing on the Sabbath, He even goes so far as to say, "Your accuser is Moses, on whom your hopes are set. If you believed Moses, you would believe me, for he wrote about me." (John 5:45-46, NIV) Where did Moses write about Jesus? In Deuteronomy. And why did this challenge matter? Because the weight of the Old Testament Law hinged on the Book of Deuteronomy, as we will discover.

Nearly as important, though, we must study Deuteronomy for what it reveals to us about the character of God. Remember when I said the Old Testament contains two-thirds of our revelatory understanding of God? Nowhere is that more intentionally and minutely focused than in Deuteronomy. More than that, our understanding of God as love (see 1 John 4:8) cannot simply be rooted in a New Testament-centric understanding of God. It is in Deuteronomy that He first appears to us clothed in this divine love: "The Lord did not set his affection on you and choose you because you were more numerous

---

[1] John Monson, "Original Context and Canon," in *Interpreting the Old Testament Theologically*, ed. Andrew T. Abernethy (Grand Rapids, MI: Zondervan, 2018), 36.
[2] Christopher Wright, *Deuteronomy* (NIBC; Peabody, MA: Hendrickson, 1996), 1.
[3] E. Achtemeier quoted in Patrick D. Miller, *Deuteronomy* (Interpretation; Louisville: Westminster John Knox, 1990), 9.

than other peoples, for you were the fewest of all peoples. But it was because *the Lord loved you…*" (Deut. 7:7-8, NIV, emphasis added)

This becomes a repeating theme throughout the book. Obedience to God should flow from our love for Him, because He first loved us. Conversely, if we are loving God, our lives will overflow with work in His good name, a product of our obedience.

Finally, Deuteronomy offers us the most in-depth commentary of the Covenant and the Law found anywhere in scripture and, as such, it gives us the earthly model for the spiritual covenant that Jesus will come to fulfill. Understanding the Old Testament Covenant agreement, promises, and responsibilities, as well as the consequences for breaking it, offers us deeper insight into our own covenantal relationship with Christ. Likewise, Moses offers us an imperfect archetype of Jesus, Himself, a topic we will certainly study in greater detail later in this book.

Are you excited, yet? Or just overwhelmed. I know the feeling. When God invited me into Deuteronomy, I'll admit, I cringed. *Really God? This is where we're going?* Deuteronomy is a hard book to study, and it is okay to acknowledge that fact. It is hard, AND you can do it. We can do it, together! It is hard, AND the blessings He had hidden away for you within its pages are innumerable. There are precious gems buried deep in the words of Moses to the people of Israel as they stood on the brink of the Promised Land. If I could share only one thing with you, one reason, above all, to walk with me through this journey, it would be this:

> "One of them, an expert in the law, tested him with this question: 'Teacher, what is the greatest commandment in the Law?'
> Jesus replied: "'Love the Lord your God with all your heart and with all your soul and with all your mind." This is the first and greatest command. And the second is like it: "Love your neighbor as yourself." All the Law and the Prophets hang on these two commandments.'" (Matt 22:35-40, NIV)

When asked about the single, most important facet of the Law, Jesus quoted Deuteronomy. Thus, we see, the Levitical Law provides the structure, the Law of Love provides the purpose, and Jesus reconciles both to Himself through the book of Deuteronomy. If that isn't a compelling reason, I don't know what is.

How To Use This Guide

Each lesson of the 20 lessons in this Study Guide will follow the same pattern: prayer, reading, response, lesson, and personal challenge. Expect each lesson to take 30-60 minutes, depending on whether you choose the Core or Extended Reading Track (more on that below). It is *not* meant to be accomplished over 20 consecutive days, but you will be more successful if you set a schedule and keep to it. Two to four lessons per week should allow you to move through them with consistency and still allow for the length of some readings.

If you are leading a small group study, you can tailor the lessons to your length of time, but a couple common options would be to do two lessons per week for ten weeks, or three lessons per week for seven weeks. More than this might be difficult for participants to complete, as the lessons are in-depth and will require a significant investment of time. Encourage your participants that Deuteronomy is a hard book to study and their investment is worthwhile! You can also encourage them to use the Core Track for reading, as the lessons will grow directly out of those passages. The Expanded Track is wonderful for a full survey of Deuteronomy, but not necessary for the study.

Prayer

Each day will begin with a reminder to begin your study time in prayer. Prayer is such a critical component of our time with God that we cannot risk forgetting it. Jesus promised, "Ask and it will be given to you; seek and you will find; knock and the door will be opened to you." (Matt.7:7, NIV) But it is prayer that unlocks the door; otherwise, we are simply peering through the windows, able to see shadowed forms within, but failing to enter fully into the Word. So important is it to begin your time with God in prayer that I've included a line for you to initial each day before continuing the lesson.

Prayer is a deeply personal and intimate expression of your relationship with God, so I have not defined how or for what you should pray. That is not for me to say. However, I know for some, myself included, prayer can sometimes feel daunting. Those who do not have a gift for it find the practice challenging. With that, please know that

God hears and welcomes all prayers, from the simplest request to the most complex and theologically sound. Whatever your prayer, please don't fail to open your study each day with one. I genuinely believe that this is the key to unlocking a deeper understanding of God's Word.

Reading

This study guide is meant to be a 20-lesson exploration of the book of Deuteronomy, including an introduction and history, a study of its component parts, and a consideration of its wider themes. However, at thirty-four chapters in length, this means that our reading will exceed the traditional one-chapter-per-lesson approach of most Bible studies.

I encourage you to embrace this challenge, but if it seems too all-consuming, don't panic. Each day will offer a *Core Track*, a series of verses that will relate directly to the day's lesson, as well as an *Extended Track*, which will keep you on track to complete Deuteronomy during our time together. Feel free to choose whichever track will work best for your study time.

Response

As you approach each day's reading, you'll be asked to consider what part of the scripture spoke most deeply to your spirit and why, or what the scripture meant to you. You will do this each day *before* beginning the structured lesson. Reading the Word should not only fuel our spirit, it should challenge our minds. Perhaps you've never heard this before, but even the writer of Hebrews advised his listeners, "You are like babies who need milk and cannot eat solid food." (Hebrews 5:12, NIV) How do we move from milk to solid food? By grappling closely with and engaging the Word as we read it.

Lesson

After you have prayed, read, and responded, we will begin the day's lesson. Each lesson will consist of some reading (commentary) and some questions designed to encourage you to dig deeper, to explore, and to consider how the scripture can be interpreted and applied. Often, you will be sent on a treasure hunt of related scripture, seeing how the core verses of the day's lesson relate to Jesus' ministry, the history of Israel, or the exhortations of the New Testament writers.

Personal Challenge

Finally, each day will end with a Personal Challenge. In some cases, the challenge will come as a direct result of the scripture we have been reading and in some cases I will encourage you to draw your day's study together in a personally applicable way. In either case, I encourage you to begin your next day's study by reviewing the previous day's Personal Challenge and asking how it has impacted you. This will also help remind you of the previous day's study, an encapsulated review.

A Note on Translations

Lessons will utilize either the NASB or the NIV Bible versions. The NASB is an extremely literal translation and has an easily-utilized concordance for word study, while the NIV is an extremely accurate thematic approach and often offers a version that is both easier to read and to understand. If the translation used will impact the lesson, I will make a special note which version would be most useful; otherwise, either version will be sufficient. If you choose to use an alternative version for your reading, please be aware that word-for-word translations may be inaccurate. This shouldn't impact your understanding of individual lessons but could cause some minor confusion if you're not aware of it. Lesson 5, in particular, will rely on multiple translations to ensure a clear understanding of the text.

Lesson 1 – Orientation to Deuteronomy

Prayer

Please open in prayer and initial here. _____

Reading

Core Track: Deuteronomy 1:1-5

Extended Track: Deuteronomy 1:1-5

Response

Take a few moments to think about the text you read today, though it was quite short. (Some questions to get you started today: What stands out to you or immediately captures your attention? Is there anything you don't understand? Are you familiar with all of the locations described and their significance?)

Lesson

Before we really dive into Deuteronomy, it is critically important that we know some key components of its history. To position ourselves to best understand it, we must first see its place within the larger canon. The narrative story of the history of the world begins in Genesis with Creation, but quickly narrows in focus to a single man, Abraham, and his descendants. In a near-unbroken chain of events, we track closely with this family throughout the remainder of Genesis and, ultimately, through Exodus, Leviticus, and Numbers.

Read Numbers 36:13, Deuteronomy 1:1, Deuteronomy 34:1, and Joshua 1:1-2. In all cases, where is the nation of Israel currently located?

Deuteronomy does not move the story forward either narratively or in a locational sense. So, what purpose does it serve? In essence, Deuteronomy takes a pause in the previously established narrative arc of the History of Israel that began in Genesis and will continue, again, almost uninterrupted, through 2 Chronicles. This pause comes at a critical juncture. Turn to the map on page 123 of this workbook. Identify the Salt Sea (also known as the Dead Sea) on the map and slide your finger just north until you find Jericho. Now, head east (to the right) until you cross the Jordan River. If you continued east, you'll find Mt. Nebo, the place of Moses' death. Draw a large circle around Mt. Nebo. If you look just to the southwest of the Salt Sea, you'll see Kadesh-Barnea, a location we'll consider in just a moment.

After forty years of wandering in the desert, the Nation of Israel stands, at last, on the cusp of the Promised Land. But they have stood in this place once before.

Read Numbers 13:25-14:4, then describe what took place in your own words. Take special note of where Israel was located at that time (see 13:26).

The importance of Deuteronomy lies in this *thematic* location.

Remember, where was Israel located at the start of Deuteronomy?

Where were they in Numbers 13?

Once again, after forty years of wandering, Israel is on the cusp of entering into the Promised Land, though this time in a different *physical* location. The spies are ready to go out. The people are armed. But will the outcome be different this time? Will their faith hold? Will they believe in God for their victory, or will they once again fall prey to their fear?

Imagine God had promised you your heart's desire but asked you to wait for it to be fulfilled. One year, five years, ten years pass, and still it stands unanswered. Perhaps this isn't difficult for you; perhaps you are in the midst of just such a time right now. More time passes, and still it is unfulfilled.

Write tomorrow's date on the line. _____

This is the day. God has said He will bring to pass what He has promised. How do you feel? What have you learned as you waited? What would you want to say to God, now, only moments from fulfillment? What would you want to say to others about God?

The Hebrew name for this book comes from the opening words in chapter one, verse one: "These are the words…" In Hebrew, they are *elleh haddebarim*, sometimes shortened to *debarim*, and the Torah calls this book *Devarim*. (In English, *Deuteronomy* literally means *the second law*, which arose from an early mistranslation of the Hebrew into the Greek, likely arising from Deuteronomy 17:18.)

You see, Israel's day had come. And these are the words that Moses spoke over them.

Personal Challenge

Consider again our thought experiment as we wait on the Lord to answer our heart's desire. What are you waiting on the Lord to answer right now in your life?

Name it here, and then pray over it, as if it will be fulfilled tomorrow.

Read Daniel 10:12. Let the impact and weight of the angel's words settle over what you have just written.

When were Daniel's words first heard?

When were your words first heard, dear one? Rest assured, it is no different. God hears you, even in the midst of the desert, and He will answer.

Lesson 2 – Fear or Faith

Prayer

    Please open in prayer and initial here. _____

Reading

    Core Track: Deuteronomy 1:20-45

    Extended Track: Deuteronomy 1:6-2:1

Response

    Remember, this is your chance to respond to the text, jot down any notes, ask questions, etc. What struck you, what confused you, etc?

Lesson

    This lesson continues the one we began yesterday with our reading in Numbers 13-14. In fact, Moses begins his oration by giving a play-by-play history of the events that have brought the nation of Israel here, to this place, on the banks of the Jordan, about to enter into the Promised Land. Remember, a journey that should have taken eleven days has now taken them forty years and cost an entire generation their lives. They weren't wandering aimlessly in the desert, lost, as if they didn't know where the Promised Land was located. No, this wandering was a punishment.

In your own words, why, specifically, were the Israelites being punished?

In short, the Israelites allowed their fear to *overcome* their faith. Fear is an emotion; it is one of those things that wells up within us when we face obstacles or odds that seem overwhelming. It is important to note that fear *as an emotion* is neither good nor bad. Emotions are red flags to our brains: "Hey, pay attention. This could hurt." But when fear overcomes faith, it goes from being an emotion to an action, and fear *as an action* is where the Israelites failed. Fear as an action becomes disobedience.

We often allow fear to control our actions. We fear that we won't have enough money, so we fail to tithe. The result: disobedience. We fear what people will think of us if we stand up for Jesus. The result: disobedience. We fear losing our sense of security, so we don't follow where God has called us. The result: disobedience.

When have you let fear control your actions? What was the result?

My second son was a complete surprise, and not a welcome one. The Plan™ had called for one child. Now four years old, he was within a year of kindergarten. I could soon leave the stay-at-home-mom stage behind, recapturing my own identity instead of being defined only by my role as a mother. I was ready. I was counting down the days. And then, all of a sudden, I was starting over. Starting over with sleepless nights and diapers. Starting over with five more years of staying home. Starting over with sinking my entire identity and purpose into another tiny human. I was overwhelmed by fear. Fear of what this baby would cost me. Fear of waiting five more years to have a life outside of motherhood. Fear of losing myself completely in the long wait to be just me again.

And my fear turned to disobedience. I was angry with God. The words of the Israelites resonated in my mind and poured from my lips: "Because the Lord hates us, He has brought us out of the land of Egypt to deliver us into the hand of the Amorites to destroy us." (Deut. 1:27, NASB) "Because the Lord hates me, He has made me have another child."

I later learned that thematically, Egypt represents self-sufficiency. Anytime you read about Egypt, especially in the Old Testament, you can almost automatically equate it with the theme of self-sufficiency. (See, for example, Abraham going to Egypt during the famine in Canaan in Genesis 12. Notice, also, how his fear bred disobedience.)

The alternative, of course, is relying on God to be your sufficiency, but that takes faith. It takes believing in something you can't quite see or hold. It takes stepping out even in the midst of fear and holding fast to the promise. "He has brought us out of our own self-sufficiency and into a daily need for faith in His provision." Literally, God called them out of Egypt, into the desert, where they relied daily on His sufficiency in the form of manna and quail.

Fear and faith cannot live side by side; one will always win. Why? Because both of them call out action. As much as fear calls us to disobedience, faith will call us to obedience.

When have you let faith control your actions? What was the result?

So how do we fight fear and build faith?

Reread Deut. 1:30-31, then read Psalm 77:11. What do these passages suggest as a method for fighting back against fear?

I love Peter. He is just a hot mess, a wreck of a human being, a failure time and time again. Pompous and proud, brash and loud; he reminds me a lot of myself. But what I think I love most about Peter is how often his fear overcomes his faith. He gives us such a poignant example of how often stepping into faith can quickly turn to fleeing in fear. He is literally walking on the surface of the water and instead of marveling at the miracle, he looks to the waves. How often do I do the same?

Read Luke 22:54-62. How do you think Peter felt as he wept?

Read Luke 22:31-32. What promise did Jesus give Peter in His prayer for him?

Are you facing an overwhelming fear right now? Is God calling you to walk in faith and you're not sure whether you have the strength to step out of the boat? Are your eyes on the waves instead of on the Wave-Maker? As the Nation of Israel stood on the banks of the Jordan River, Moses was calling them. Would they step out in faith, or would they run in fear?

Personal Challenge:

My second son was born on Mother's Day. God knew how I felt about being pregnant. He knew what I was struggling with. He knew my fears, selfish and small as they were. And He answered all of them in His perfect timing. The moment that baby was laid into my arms, I fell in love with him. He's in school, now, and not only do I love him more each day, God has gone even farther. I haven't lost myself; He has opened paths to allow my ministry to grow and flourish over the last several years. He has taken me deeper and loved me harder than I ever could have imagined in the midst of all of my anger and bitter resentment.

Read John 21. How did Peter react to seeing Jesus?

What were Jesus' parting words to Peter?

Have you been overwhelmed by fear? Has it caused you to walk in disobedience? Following Peter's model, reassert your love for God. Ask for forgiveness and for the strength to walk in faith. Declare your intention to follow Him.

Lesson 3 – Promises

Prayer

Please open in prayer and initial here. _____

Reading

Core Track: Deuteronomy 2:2-2:22
Extended Track: Deuteronomy 2:1-3:29

Response

Take a moment to respond to the text. What verse or verses struck you in today's reading?

Lesson

God had promised a land to the Israelites. A good land. A land flowing with milk and honey. He promised this land to Abraham in Genesis 13 and again in Genesis 15, along with a nation of sons, so many that they would be as innumerable as "the dust of the earth." (Gen 13:16, NASB) But Abraham is not the only one to whom God made promises, particularly of land. Today, we will study some of the other "land promises" God made and ask ourselves how they might apply in our own lives.

Read Genesis 25:27-34 and 27:30-40. Compare and contrast these stories, making special note of how Esau felt about his birthright and his blessing and how they each were lost. What do these stories say about Esau? About Jacob? About their relationship?

Read Genesis 36:6-8. After many years spent away from each other, Jacob returns and makes amends to his brother (See Genesis 32-33). Realizing the land cannot sustain both their families, they part ways.

What two names does Genesis 36:8 give to the land where Esau settled?

Reread Deuteronomy 2:5. Who has given what to whom?

Reread Deuteronomy 2:9. Who has given what to whom in this passage?

Read Genesis 13:1-12. How does the parting of ways between Esau and Jacob reflect the parting of ways between Abraham and Lot?

Israel was not the only nation to whom God had made promises, though it is clear from the text that the choicest portion of land was probably set aside for God's chosen nation. Flip again to the map on page 123 and find the Salt Sea or the Dead Sea (remember, these are the same). Esau and his descendants were given the land of Seir, also known as Edom, just south of the Dead Sea; Lot and his descendants were given the land of Moab, also known as Ar, just east of the Dead Sea. The Israelites had to pass through both of these areas in order to reach their current location.

Reread Deuteronomy 2:4-6 and 9. This time, focus on the instructions that God gave Israel as they passed through these lands. In v. 4, God warns them to be "very _____;" in v. 5 and 9, He tells them not to "_____ them to war;" and in v. 9, He also says, "Do not _____ the Moabites." Finally, in v. 6, God requires that Israel pay for the food they eat and the water they drink while within the borders of these lands. Why do you think He asked this of them?

Personal Challenge:

We have gone to a great deal of effort to establish that God can make promises to anyone He wants, and that those promises may differ between people. Let's take a moment, now, to consider how this knowledge might affect our own lives. I think two lessons are immediately apparent:

1. What God has promised to me, He will not allow another to take or keep.
2. What God has promised to another, He will not allow me to take or keep.

Early on in my teaching and speaking career, I often felt threatened by others pursuing the same vocation. I would feel angry if another speaker was chosen instead of me. I would listen to their words with a spirit of derision, pointing out every mistake they made, contesting every thesis if it disagreed with my own. As I've grown and matured, I've begun to realize that God's plan for my ministry is not the same as His plan for another's ministry, and there is a place for all of them within His kingdom. Like Paul's analogy of one body with many parts, the areas of ministry that I am best suited to serve are not always the same areas that a group of people need to be served within.

Take a moment to think about what promises God has given you, alone. Have you ever felt that promise was threatened by another? How did you feel, think, or react?

Even as my ministry began to grow, I would often look at the ministry of others with a sense of jealousy or covetousness, wondering why mine couldn't be as big as theirs, as deep as theirs. I asked God why He was opening doors for them but not for me. If you did only the Core Reading today, read Deuteronomy 3:12-17; if you did the Extended Reading today, then reread this passage to remind yourself of its contents.

Before they ever crossed the Jordan, some of the Israelites had already come into their inheritance. Some of them were already being permitted to settle their families and their herds, while others had yet to come into their promises. So it can be with us, as well. We look to the right or the left and see those who are already dwelling within God's promises for their lives, and we wonder why we haven't come into our Promised Land yet.

Tread carefully in these places. They are not our promises, not our lands to possess. God will not give them to us any more than He will give away to others the things He has promised to us.

Have you coveted another's promises fulfilled? If so, take a moment to ask God for forgiveness. Repent and read Jeremiah 29:11-13. Declare your faith in God's promise and plans for your life.

Lesson 4 - Remember

Prayer

    Please open in prayer and initial here. _____

Reading

    Core Track: Deuteronomy 4:9, 32-40

    Extended Track: Deuteronomy 4:1-4:43

Response

    Take a moment to respond to the text.

Lesson

    Two lessons ago, I shared about how I allowed my fear to control my actions while I was pregnant with my second son. To this day, the redemption of that time is one of the greatest acts that God has committed in my life. He delivered me from the bitter anger and resentment of those weeks and months and replaced my heart of stone with a heart of flesh (Ez. 36:26). He gave me a heart of tenderness and love towards my son, as well as a heart that repented of my disobedience and returned again to God. But beyond the miracle of a restored heart - a restored soul - this story holds a miracle of a restored body, as well.

    Though much of the fear around this pregnancy was selfish and self-centered, some of it was rooted in genuine concern for my well-being. After my first son was born, I faced complications that nearly took my life. These complications manifested themselves again with the birth of my second son and were much more severe. As the anesthesiologist struggled to find a vein that hadn't collapsed due to blood loss, I told the nurses how my vision was tunneling and darkening around the edges. My last conscious memory is of a voice somewhere above my head swearing, then yelling, "We have to get her into surgery *now*!"

> *Read Numbers 25:1-9 and Deuteronomy 4:3-4. Describe the literal life-threatening event that Israel had faced, how it was stopped, and how many died. Who survived and why? How long ago do you think this event took place (hint: look at Deuteronomy 3:29)?*

When Moses exhorts Israel to remember God for the sake of their very lives (Deut. 4:4), he is not exaggerating, and this event is not very far removed from their present, maybe even as little as a few days to a few weeks.

> *Reread Deuteronomy 4:32-39 and list all of the things Moses is encouraging the Israelites to remember.*

> *Why do you think Moses is reminding the Israelites of all that God has done for them?*

Memory is fickle. Science tells us that memory originates with sensory perceptions; the experience, itself, then is coded to short-term memory. Short-term memory holds a limited quantity of sensory perceptions for a limited period of time, usually no more than seven specific memories for no more than thirty seconds[4]. Information that is not then coded into long-term memory is lost. So how does the short-term information get transferred to long-term storage? Through repetition. The more it is repeated or utilized, the more likely it is to be retained.

---

[4] Richard C. Mohs "How Human Memory Works" 8 May 2007. HowStuffWorks.com.
<https://science.howstuffworks.com/life/inside-the-mind/human-brain/human-memory.htm> 29 May 2019

Think of your phone number and how quickly you can rattle it off. Or your birth date, social security number, and address. These pieces of identifying information are ones that we use on an almost-daily basis. I bet if you thought about it for a moment, you could even come up with your childhood phone number or address, though you may not have used it in years. Repetition codes these memories into long-term storage, where they can stay almost indefinitely. Moses' exhortations to remember the works of God are the modern, scientific equivalent of calling upon Israel to recode their short-term memories into long-term memories.

In addition to recoding them into long-term memories, what other purposes can remembering serve, both individually and corporately?

Conversely, when we do not spend time intentionally meditating on the good things God has done for us, we can easily lose sight of Him in our lives.

What great things has God done in your life that you would do well to remember?

After six hours in surgery, I woke up again. Honestly, I wasn't sure that I would. With my background in emergency response, I had a very clear sense of what I was experiencing in my final moments of consciousness and what those symptoms probably meant. My first coherent thought was simple but profound: "God's not done with me, yet." If He had been, I don't believe my eyes would ever have opened again on this side of eternity.

Read Psalm 23:4. How does this verse weave into our theme of remembrance? (Need a hint? How does knowing God is with us interweave with remembering what He has done?)

Personal Challenge

When we have lost sight of God, remembering what He has done is a good place to begin looking for Him again.

Read Psalm 77:11-15. What is David remembering about God? How do verses 13-15 reflect the verses in our core reading today?

One of my favorite passages comes from 2 Chronicles 20, which follows King Jehoshaphat as he prepares for a battle he cannot possibly win. Afraid, he resolves to seek the Lord and asks the whole country to fast with him (2 Chron. 20:3), then he begins to pray.

Read 2 Chronicles 20:5-12. What mighty things does Jehoshaphat remember God doing on behalf of their country?

I was first introduced to this passage by the apologist Ravi Zacharias[5]. In it, he calls out three critical phases in this prayer, summarized by the triplet, "Are you not, did you not, will you not?" In your Bible, I encourage you to circle each of these phrases (see v. 6, 7, and 12). Jehoshaphat begins by extolling the very character of God, His power, and His dominion over all the earth (are you not). Then, he remembers the things God has done for the nation of Israel (did you not). Finally, he presents his request with faith that God will provide an answer (will you not).

In the midst of a crisis, it can be difficult to remember the things God has done, so today I'm going to invite you to craft your own prayer as a touchstone against future need. Use the space below to create your own version of Jehoshaphat's prayer.

Are you not...

---

[5] Despite his personal shortcomings, I believe his teaching on this topic remains viable and worthwhile.

Did you not…

Perhaps you are in the midst of a great need or are waiting on a promise of God to be fulfilled. If so, feel free to continue this prayer through to completion in the space below.

Will you not…

God is faithful, and your own life can be the proof of that statement. When God fulfills a promise, write it down. Proclaim it. Testify to it. Praise Him for it. Force that short-term coding to convert to a long-term memory. Don't stop declaring it.

Write out Deuteronomy 4:9 and spend some time praising God for what He has done.

Lesson 5 – The Fear of the Lord

Prayer

Please open in prayer and initial here. _____

Reading

Core Track: Deuteronomy 5:1-5, 22-33

Extended Track: Deuteronomy 4:44-5:33

Response

Take a moment to respond to the text. Pay particular attention to today's topic – The Fear of the Lord – and draw some conclusions of your own before beginning the lesson.

Lesson

Scholars divide Deuteronomy in a number of different ways, but one of the most common is by the three speeches of Moses, each with a clearly defined purpose, beginning, and end. Our last lesson wrapped up the first speech of Moses (Deut. 1:6-4:43) and today we begin our look at the second speech of Moses, which will take us through the next twenty-four chapters of the book.

Incidentally, other scholars suggest that Deuteronomy follows a chiastic structure – a reflective or crisscross pattern where early parts of the text are echoed in later parts. (For example, chapters 1-3 could be called "A Look Backwards" while chapters 31-34 could be called "A Look Forwards."[6]) Feeling a little lost? Don't worry, we'll come back to this chiastic structure in a later lesson. For now, just know that as we leave Moses' first speech behind, we'll be looping back around to it later. Now, on to today's lesson.

---

[6] Bill Arnold and Bryan E. Beyer, *Encountering the Old Testament* (Grand Rapids: Baker Books, 1999), 143

Read Proverbs 1:7. How do you think that the fear of the Lord can lead to knowledge and/or wisdom?

Look up the word "fear" in a dictionary and write the definition below. Think up a short list of words that mean the same thing to you, then look up a list of synonyms for fear and add any more that strike you.
Definition: My Words: Additional Words:

In Hebrew, the word for *fear* is *yir'ah* and the word for *afraid* is similar, *yare'*, showing the shared etymology between them. In some cases, it means exactly what you wrote above; words that may have included *dread*, *terror*, or *cowardice*. In other cases, however, this exact same word can mean *reverence*, *awe*, or even *worship*. To make matters worse, sometimes different versions of the Bible translate this word in different ways.

Read 2 Kings 17:28-41 in an NASB or ESV translation, then read it again in an NIV or NLT translation. What two words are used to express very different approaches to God? Do you think they are truly interchangeable? How does your understanding of the reading change based on the translation?

Ultimately, the takeaway from our text today is that Moses and the Israelites were having two very different conversations. Moses was trying to teach them to revere and respect God; seeing His manifest power, they, on the other hand, were simply terrified.

Reread Deuteronomy 5:22-27. Why were they afraid and what did the Israelites do about their fear?

Reread Deuteronomy 5:2-4. How does this differ from the relationship that God was actively seeking with them?

It is critical to remember that this covenant was, indeed, made with their "fathers," twice over: both their ancestral fathers, Abraham, Isaac, and Jacob, but also in Exodus 20, which Moses is referencing here. At that time most of those present during this speech would have been children, sitting under the authority of their literal, earthly fathers. After forty years of wandering in the desert, the Israelites about to enter the Promised Land are a whole new generation, save for three: Moses, Joshua, and Caleb.

In light of this fact, what do you think Moses means when he declares God's personal covenant with them in verses 2-4?

Okay, stick with me, because we're about to get a little bit theological. The Covenant Promise was originally made to Abraham, who was not a nation in and of himself, but an individual. Likewise, it was reiterated to his descendants - Isaac, Jacob, and Joseph - as an individual promise. Israel is now a great nation, the nation that God promised would come out of Abraham. But it is still a nation made up of *individual people*. This matters because God's covenant was not just with the nation as a whole, but with each individual person within that nation. His covenant is *corporate* and *personal*. Even today, God desires a *corporate* relationship with us (within the body of the church) as well as a *personal* relationship with us.

Have you heard the saying that going to McDonalds doesn't make you a hamburger any more than going to church makes you a Christian? We must have a personal relationship with God, to know him intimately, "face to face," in order to revere and worship him. But the role of the church in walking out our faith is crucial, as well, for fellowship, for instruction, for exhortation, and for accountability. It is through the church, too, that God has called us to care for others, to spread the gospel message, and to go into all the world.

Israel let their fear of the Lord lead them to taking a step back, a step away. When we are more afraid of what God will do *to us* than of what God will do *through us*, we step back, as well.

Personal Challenge:

As we discussed in Lesson 2, fear can draw a straight line to disobedience if we are not careful. Like Peter, Timothy, too, struggled with fear and, as he was pastoring the church at Ephesus, Paul wrote to him, encouraging and exhorting him to remain steadfast.

> *Read 2 Timothy 1:7. Paul contrasts Timothy's "timidity" with three things God has given us instead. (Note that some translations use "fear" or "cowardice" in place of "timidity.") What are these three things and how do you think they help us overcome timidity, fear or cowardice, especially in regards to our relationship with God?*

I think our fear of God can sometimes feel different than the fear the Israelites felt towards Him. Maybe we don't tremble before Him, but there are ways we show our fear that are more subtle. There have been times in my life that I have not trusted that God truly wanted the best for me. Times when I have doubted that "all things work together for good," (Romans 8:28) or when I have doubted that "'I know the plans I have for you,' declares the Lord. 'Plans to prosper you and not to harm you, plans to give you a hope and a future.'" (Jeremiah 29:11) In the midst of whatever trials I have been facing, I have forgotten that they have been to "produce perseverance." (James 1:3) Instead, my fear of what God was doing *to me*, the pain of living through the trial, overwhelmed my faith in what He could do *through me*.

The fastest way to lose your reverence for God is to approach Him second-hand. When Israel called upon Moses - and later called upon the High Priest - to approach God in their place, they lost the personal relationship with Him that would have ensured their love for and trust in His perfect purposes. Moreover, that loss led them on a direct path into sin. So, God sent us a new High Priest, one who would never die, one who, instead of standing in the gap between us and God *became* the gap between us and God, closing it forever.

Read Hebrews 12:18-24. How does the way in which we can approach God via Jesus differ from how the Israelites approached Him in the wilderness? (Hint: also look up Hebrews 4:14-16 and 10:19-22.)

In Acts 2, Jesus sends the Holy Spirit to the convened church, as promised. Now, not only do we have God above and Jesus beside, but also the Spirit within.

Read 1 Corinthians 2:11-12. How close can we come to God? By what route?

Do you feel a sense of being "face to face" with God today? I admit, I often struggle to find myself in intimate communion with any facet of the Trinity. Their ways feel so above and beyond my ways, Their thoughts so far above and beyond my thoughts, so spiritual while I am mired in such fleshliness, it feels hard to find Them. But that is not Their heart towards me, towards you. Their desire is to be as close as our own heartbeat, beating in time to Their ways and Their thoughts.

Invite God, Jesus, and the Holy Spirit in today. Spend some time in prayer thanking Them for their intimate and personal love for you, and ask how you can walk in closer step with Them.

Lesson 6 – Hear, O Israel

Prayer

　　Please open in prayer and initial here. _____

Reading

　　Core Track: Deuteronomy 6:4-12, 6:23

　　Extended Track: Deuteronomy 6:1-6:25

Response

　　Take a moment to respond to the text. Remember, if you are on the Core Track, respond directly to what you read by drawing your own conclusions. If you are on the Extended Track, make note of and respond to any portion that particularly struck you, even if it is outside our Core reading.

Lesson

　　Remember our discussion in the introduction about how every writer in the New Testament was, first and foremost, culturally and historically Jewish? Nowhere is that more apparent than in our reading of Deuteronomy 6, and if there is any chapter where those of you doing the Core Track should take the extra time to read the entire Extended reading, this is it. It is here, in chapter 6, that we see the foundation of a loving God laid in a way that we can directly relate to our New Testament understanding of Him.

　　First, we will address a key passage that would have shaped every New Testament writer's understanding of God.

Reread Deuteronomy 6:4-5. Do these words feel familiar and if so, why?

This section is the opening lines of one of the most well-known Jewish prayers of all time, the *Shema* (shä-mah' or shuh-MAH). The *Shema* includes a number of scriptures from the *Torah*, the Hebrew Holy Book which consists of the first five books of our Old Testament.

Write out the names of the first five books of the Old Testament. Think about what you know of them and why they would be important to modern Jews. Why are they important to modern Christians, too? How does sharing this heritage bring us closer together?

Read Ephesians 2:11-21. In Paul's eyes, what is the relationship between Jew and Gentile (note that he is talking about Messianic Jews and Converted Gentiles: Jews and Gentiles who have come to know Christ). How do these verses change or enhance your answer to the previous question?

The *Shema* is a twice-daily Jewish recitation, a liturgy, that is still in use today. It begins with Deuteronomy 6:4-5, then continues with 6:6-9. From there, it jumps to Deuteronomy 11:13-21, then finishes in Numbers 15:37-41. There are also three blessings which are spoken, two before and one after. These thank God for His creation, His revelation, and His redemption. I don't know about you, but these are themes which seem to resonate in my own walk with Christ, today. Amazing how thousands of years have passed, the revelation of God has expanded to include Jesus, and yet, these words still feel timeless.

While we are here, planting ourselves deep in this rich cultural and historical prayer, I want to draw your attention to two specific words in the opening lines of the *Shema*. The name *Shema*, in fact, is in reference to the very first word of the prayer: *hear*. *Shema* means *hear*.

What does it mean to you to hear? Is there a difference between listening and hearing?

Strong's Concordance suggests a more emphatic meaning for this word, to hear: "to hear intelligently (often with implication of attention, obedience, etc)" (Strong's H8085). Read James 1:19-25, focusing especially on verse 22, and Hebrews 2:1. How do these verses enrich your understanding of the concept of hearing?

While this first word points us in a very specific direction, the second word warranting a moment more of our attention is one that can be sticky and troublesome if not properly understood. Verse 4 ends with the phrase, "the Lord is one," and if you've ever read that and paused to wonder what it means, we might be kindred spirits. One of my favorite things while reading Scripture is to run across an odd phrase or word and then chase that rabbit trail all the way to the den until I can understand it. This one is no different, though, fortunately, fairly simple, especially compared to some of the words we'll look at later in Deuteronomy.

Before I give you an explanation, take a moment to grapple with this phrase and word, "one." What do you think it means?

Read Deuteronomy 6:4 in the KJV and NLT versions if you have them available. Does this help you pinpoint the meaning of the phrase? How so?

The Jewish Study Bible translates this phrase as, "The Lord is our God, the Lord alone,[7]" and some more esoteric translations even say, "The Lord is The Unique."

Read Exodus 15:11. How does this verse relate to the concept of the Lord as "one?"

---

[7] Adele Berlin, Marc Zvi Brettler, and Micheal Fishbane, *The Jewish Study Bible* (Oxford, England: Oxford University Press, 2004), 379

Now that we have a clear understanding of the Jewish *Shema*, let's turn our attention to the remainder of our Core passage, verses 5-12.

We'll come back in a moment to verse 5, but for now, I want you to take a moment to notice and appreciate the clear line Moses is drawing between the feeling of love Israel should have towards God (v. 5) and the actions they should take because of it (v.6-12). Even the very word *shema*, to listen, means so much more: to listen *and* obey. Remember our lesson about faith and fear and how they will always be in opposition because they both call out action. Love is another one of those "action" words. In Bob Goff's *Love Does*, he writes, "…love is never stationary. In the end, love doesn't just keep thinking about it or keep planning for it. Simply put: love does.[8]" Love calls out a responding and correlating action, and Moses is suggesting any number of them to Israel.

Write out all the things Moses is asking Israel to do in verses 6-12.

Interestingly, we can also link this part of the lesson back to several previous lessons.

First, let's review Lesson 4 – Remembering. How do Moses' words in Deuteronomy 6:6-12 recall our lesson on both the importance of remembering and the methodology (Deut. 4:32-39, p. 27)?

Next, let's review a small portion of Lesson 5 – The Fear of the Lord, on the topic of God's covenantal promises being both corporate and personal (p. 33). Refer to your list of actions in the question above and note in parenthesis beside each action whether it is more personal or more corporate. For example, if you wrote, "Impress them on your children," you might mark it with (corporate) because it requires a corporate response; whereas if you wrote, "Write them on your doorframe," you might mark it with (personal) because it is an action you can take alone. Feel free to mark them in whatever feels most appropriate to you.

---

[8] Bob Goff, *Love Does* (Nashville, TN: Thomas Nelson, 2012), xvi

Personal Challenge:

One of the things I find so fascinating about God's love is that it is not transactional. It is not a result of something earned but is something freely given. Before Israel had lifted a sword or fought a single battle in the Promised Land, God already loved them. In fact, given their recent and on-going disobedience, His ever-lasting love is ever more miraculous. In *Liturgy of the Ordinary*, Tish Harrison Warren says, "It's remarkable that when the Father declares at Jesus' baptism, 'This is my beloved Son, with whom I am well pleased,' Jesus hasn't yet done much of anything that many would find impressive. He hasn't yet healed anyone or resisted Satan in the wilderness. He hasn't yet been crucified or resurrected. It would make more sense if the Father's proud announcement came after seeing something grand and glorious…[9]" And yet, this was the moment God chose.

So it is with us. God's love is the foundation of our identity. Everything we do should flow outward from that cornerstone, leveling the walls of our lives and keeping our roofs from leaking.

When asked to name the greatest commandment, Jesus spoke words that should feel familiar after today's lesson.

Read Matthew 22:36-40. According to Jesus, what is the greatest commandment? What is the second greatest?

Write out Deuteronomy 6:5, the text Jesus is quoting in his response in Matthew.

Jesus had a lot to choose from in answering this question. He could have chosen any of the Ten Commandments, or any of the six-hundred-eleven other rules that were later added to comprise The Law of Jesus' time. He chose this one.

Write as many "rules" or "laws" of the Old Testament as you can remember. Why do you think none of these were deemed by Jesus as "the most important?"

---

[9] Tish Harrison Warren, *Liturgy of the Ordinary: Sacred Practices in Everyday Life* (Downers Grove, IL: InterVarsity Press, 2016), 16.

Jesus' answer is genius in many ways. First, by invoking Moses he would have effectively silenced most of the Pharisees, who prided themselves on their careful consideration of Mosaic Law, both in its original, Ten Commandment form and in its later, expanded form. By establishing such credentials within his argument, he backed his detractors into a corner, forcing them to either agree with him or deny Moses' place as the greatest prophet in Jewish history. Second, it encompasses by its very nature at least the Ten Commandments, if not all of the Law.

Read Exodus 20:1-17 and jot a quick word or two below to remind you of each of the Ten Commandments. Beside each command, note whether it falls under the umbrella of loving God or loving your neighbor.

	Command	*God or Neighbor*
1.		
2.		
3.		
4.		
5.		
6.		
7.		
8.		
9.		
10.		

Arguably, loving others is, on its own, a further act of loving God. If we love them because God commanded us to – especially when we don't really *want* to love them – we show even more love for God through our submission to Him.

Read Ephesians 2:8-10 and paraphrase these verses in your own words. What does Paul say should flow out of the saving grace we have received? What drives us to do this?

Lesson 7 – No Other Gods

Prayer

Please open in prayer and initial here. _____

Reading

Core Track: Deuteronomy 7:2-11; 8:11-20

Extended Track: Deuteronomy 7:1-8:20

Response

Take a moment to respond to the text. Consider how it relates to our closing exercise of yesterday, reviewing the Ten Commandments.

Lesson

In Lesson 5, we discussed that there were a number of different ways that scholars divide or outline Deuteronomy. The Second Speech of Moses, as Andrew Hill and John Walton[10] call it, extends from Deuteronomy 4:44 all the way to 28:68; however, the bulk of this speech is roughly from chapter 5 to chapter 26. It is formatted specifically around the Ten Commandments, which Hill and Walton call the *Decalogue*, beginning with a review in 5:6-21, then elaborated upon, point by point, throughout the next twenty chapters. Our last lesson, this lesson, and the next lesson will all place us within this framework and encompass Moses' illumination of the first of the Ten Commandments, which began in chapter 6 and will continue to chapter 11.

---

[10] Andrew E. Hill and John H. Walton, *A Survey of the Old Testament* 3rd Edition (Grand Rapids: Zondervan, 2009), 164

What is the First Commandment? Without looking it up, see if you can remember it. If not, glance back at Deuteronomy 5:7. Why do you think Moses devotes six chapters - almost one-third the length of this speech - to this particular command?

Deuteronomy is not only a book of small laws, it is a book of big concepts. This is why we spend time understanding its structure. If we only read individual verses and rules, we risk missing the forest for the trees. Grand, sweeping themes permeate every chapter, spiraling again and again back to the same places.

What are some major themes of Deuteronomy you've already identified through your reading? Consider the topics of some of our lessons and whether you've seen them pop up again in later readings.

Understanding the Big Ideas of Deuteronomy allows the reader to dig deeper than just the surface, it allows a glimpse into the very heart and character of God. When Deuteronomy 5:7 declares, "You shall have no other gods before me," God is revealing a great truth of His mightiness. It is interesting that most versions translate it as *before*, when a truer translation would actually be *besides*. In fact, even as they use the word *before*, most versions note in the text that an alternative translation would be *besides*.

How does reading this verse using "besides" instead of "before" change the meaning of the text?

Keeping in mind our Big Ideas theme, how does today's reading - either Core or Extended - reflect this better understanding of the First Commandment? If our thesis statement of these chapters is God's absolute sovereignty, how does every verse point back to this?

The risk of idolatry in the ancient culture described in Deuteronomy was significant. Many different beliefs permeated the lands that the Jewish people had come from, traveled through, and now were about to enter into. Egyptian religion encompassed no fewer than two thousand different gods and goddesses. The culture of Canaan, the land they were entering, was deeply entwined with many versions of Ba'al and Ashera, as well as others. Each family would have had an altar in their own home on which would have stood carvings of these false gods and goddesses (see Genesis 31:19, 30-35 for an example of this practice). Idols: the fanciest of which were burnished with precious metals and decorated with jewels, the most modest of which would at least have had some indication of their value, whatever the family could afford, humble as it might have been.

The Jewish people had already brushed up against idolatry during their long journey, and paid a heavy price for their faithlessness.

Read Exodus 32. Paraphrase what happened in this chapter, including what happened and what the consequences were. Sum up in one sentence the cost of going after false gods.

Another of our Big Ideas of Deuteronomy is the on-going exhortation to *remember*. In remembering the consequences of their previous sin, the nation of Israel ought to have logically concluded that chasing after false gods leads to death. But did they learn?

In Lesson 4 we discussed Numbers 25:1-9. Reread these verses to remind yourself of their content, then paraphrase what happened, including the consequences. Did this take place before or after the previous bout of idolatry?

Perhaps Moses continues to exhort the people to *remember* because they are so abysmally bad at it.

Personal Challenge:

Today, we are somewhat less likely to be taken in by false gods in the form of *physical* idols. However, we remain as prone to faithlessness as ever before. If anything, our current culture is more insidious in its deception.

What "false gods" or idols do you think people are prone to follow today? Circle anything on your list that you, yourself, have fallen victim to.

If you are anything like me, your list probably went on until you ran out of space: money, fame, your husband or children, your work, your favorite hobby, an exceptional pastor or teacher, control of a situation, pride, etc. If I'm being honest, every item I listed would probably also get a circle. Maybe I don't struggle with it today, but I probably have at some point in the past, and will again soon. Ouch.

I think it's easy to look back and judge the people of Israel. "They saw the very glory of God, yet still they turned away…" But judgement it truly is. When I think about all the manifest ways God has revealed His glory in my life, personally, intimately, powerfully and mightily, can I really dare to claim that seeing a column of fire or of smoke would have made me one iota more likely to be faithful?

Read Deuteronomy 7:25-26. What does Moses demand that Israel do with any idol they find during their conquest of the Promised Land? Why?

If this is how God desired the idols of the Canaanites to be treated, how much more so should we treat the idols of our current culture? Depending on your translation, the words used for such things might be *an abomination, detestable, vile,* or *cursed,* and the response would be to *utterly abhor it, ban it,* or *destroy it.* These are not neutral words; these are harsh, negative words taken to their extreme. Not just *abhor it,* but **utterly** *abhor it.*

Sometimes we think we know what a word means but our understanding is only contextual. What do you think "abhor" means? After writing your definition, look it up and write the dictionary definition. Are there any other words in these verses that you are not familiar with or think you understand but want to double check? Look them up and write their definitions, as well. (Consider "abomination," "detestable," or even "utterly.")

I have a confession to make: I spent years watching a famous reality TV show about a single man or woman choosing among a bevy of possible suitors. I bet you know which one I'm talking about. At first, I loved watching it for the thrill of seeing their young love unfold. Later, it was with a more judgmental attitude, knowing it was doomed to failure for a vast variety of reasons, but almost unable to turn away. As it became more racy with each passing season, more fraught with drama, and, ultimately, so scripted that it ceased to have any claim of "reality," I realized that my initial reasons for watching it, cute and fun and sweet, had shifted towards more sardonic amusement, then, finally, disgust. Why did I continue watching this thing that added no value to my life, that actively advocated lifestyles that I neither agreed with nor approved of, that had sunk so deeply into lustful depravity that I couldn't even see a hint of redemption in it?

In studying this passage, I realized that, for whatever reason, this show had become something I had brought into my home, treated as an idol ("There's a new episode!"), and then been taken in by. It was a detestable thing, an abomination that I was supposed to be abhorring, and instead I had given it a place in my life. I know I'm not alone in this.

What has seeped into your life, shaping it in new ways that don't focus first, even solely, on God? Don't let shame overtake you, here, but invite the Holy Spirit to help you identify these areas, then ask forgiveness for them.

What can you do right now, this moment, to turn away from these idols? Not just to scale back your attention on them but truly turn away, abhor and despise them, burn them and cleanse your life of them. Write your action steps here. You might even want to stop this study right now and go make some changes. Delete that book off your kindle, stop the DVR for that show, throw away that item that keeps enticing you.

Was this exercise difficult? Why do you think God used such strong language to describe idols and idolatry?

In Ephesians, Paul focusses not on the idols, themselves, but on the source of all idolatry. He says, "For our struggle is not against flesh and blood but against the rulers, against the powers, against the world forces of this darkness, against the spiritual forces of wickedness in the heavenly places." (Ephesians 6:12, NASB) He goes on to list the iconic parts of Spiritual Armor to help resist the insidious deceits of Satan.

Read Ephesians 6:13-18. What articles of armor does Paul recommend wearing in our battle against the enemy? Which piece of armor feels most important to you today as you seek to turn away from an idol of this world. Write it down, then pray for God to strengthen it in you.

God wants our entire worship, our entire attention, shared with no one and nothing. For many of us, to live this way would be watershed change. Our lives would never look the same. And yet, if Deuteronomy tells us anything through its recounting and remembrance of all God has done, it is that He is worthy of this kind of worship. He loved us first, before we did anything worth loving; He loves us still, even as we struggle day in and day out with sin; He loves us forever, sealed in the Book of Life for all time. He is worthy.

Lesson 8 – A Stubborn and Rebellious People

Prayer

Please open in prayer and initial here. _____

Reading

Core Track: Deuteronomy 9:4-6; 9:26-29; 10:12-17

Extended Track: Deuteronomy 9:1-10:22

Response

Take a moment to respond to the text.

Lesson

As we begin today's lesson, recall that we are still in the midst of a six-chapter lecture on the First Commandment. If you are feeling ambitious, you could read chapters six to eleven all together and see the thread of this thesis pulled all the way through in a variety of different themes; however, it is a bit much to tackle in a single lesson. It would also preclude visiting some of those valuable "trees" that are planted in the "forest" of the Big Ideas of Deuteronomy. Today will be one of those precious "tree" lessons, probably a welcome break from the "forest" lessons of the last few days; yet, it will also relate directly back to some of those larger themes we've been discussing recently.

Reread the Core Track verses in Deuteronomy 9 (9:4-6 and 26-29). Name two reasons that God gave Israel the Promised Land (see v. 4 and 28).

Moses also cautions his listeners that God did not give them the Promised Land for other reasons. In fact, three times in three verses Moses repeats himself, lest anyone miss it the first or second time.

What words repeat themselves three times over in v. 4, 5, and 6? Why do you think Moses felt it was so important to reiterate his point?

Finally, Moses caps this point with a zinger of an accusation: "…you are a stubborn people." In my notes on this chapter, I have a little arrow at this line and the words "It. Me." written, in the current popular vernacular, in the margin.

I am always amazed at how God can speak through even the most archaic language and ancient stories directly to my soul. It has been three-and-a-half thousand years since Moses lived and his words still cut straight to my heart.

Israel was stubborn in their sin, stubborn in their insistence on chasing after false gods, stubborn in their constant need to be self-sufficient (remember that Egypt *thematically* represents this need for control).

Reread Deuteronomy 9:27-29. Keeping in mind the thematic importance of Egypt ("the land from which You brought us"), what do you think might have been the "double" meaning in Moses' concern.

Israel was stubborn in many ways, but, fundamentally, all these varied forms of stubbornness sprang from one source, a desire to be self-sufficient. Independent. In control. God, on the other hand, was leading them on a journey out of self-sufficiency, out of independence and control, and into reliance on Him.

One of my favorite literary lines of all time is JRR Tolkien's iconic, "Not all those who wander are lost," from *The Fellowship of the Ring*. Israel had been wandering the desert for forty years, not because they were lost, as we established in Lesson 1, but because they were on a God-ordained pilgrimage. From the very start, they had resisted His sovereignty, resisted Moses as His messenger, resisted His plan for their flight from Egypt. Since then, although He had provided abundantly for their daily needs with miraculous clouds of manna and quail, they had remained rebellious. God gave them chance after chance to prove their faithfulness, and they failed again and again. Certainly, this seems to be the point that Moses is making in today's passage.

But does it tell the whole story? Is the history of Israel's wanderings nothing more than a litany of their sins against God, or is there something else there?

Reread Numbers 13:30 and 25:7-9. Instead of focusing on the disobedience of some, focus on the obedience of others. Who were the heroes of these stories and why?

As a whole, Israel seemed to fail again and again, but individually, there were those among the people who were getting the message. As the years in the desert passed, more and more began to figure it out. In fact, as you read the history of their wanderings throughout the book of Numbers, you can see this theme repeating itself. For every act of corporate disobedience, a few stand out as being true and obedient.

This is a powerful Old Testament example of a critical New Testament concept: sanctification.

What do you think sanctification means? After writing your definition, look it up in a dictionary and add any additional or different meanings.

To be even more specific, the journey of Israel through the wilderness is a beautiful example of the process of sanctification that Paul describes in such detail in all of his writings. It is a physical pilgrimage that reflects the spiritual pilgrimage both of the people of that time and also for ourselves, in this one.

Read 1 John 1:9 and 3:9. What do these verses promise us as believers in Christ? Have you seen this truth reflected in your life?

1 John adamantly declares several times over that those who are in Christ no longer sin. But…but what does it mean, then, that I still do? If I am in Christ and I am promised that sin can no longer live in me, then why do I continue to sin? Or, as Paul puts it, "I do not understand what I do. For what I want to do I do not do, but what I hate I do." (Romans 7:15)

Yet, here is the great paradox of our faith: if we were indeed made completely sinless by our belief in Jesus, what use would we have to live out our daily lives in pursuit of God? It is by our very failures that we are reminded, day by day, of our overwhelming need for a God of grace and mercy. That is why sanctification is a process. We stand with one foot in the heavenly places – before God as though sinless because of the blood of Jesus for our sins – but we also keep one foot on this earthly sphere. And that foot keeps getting stuck in the mud.

Personal Challenge:

I am a recovering perfectionist. I say "recovering" because I have recognized the damaging role this philosophy has played and continues to play in my life, but I haven't yet overcome it. It permeates every part of my life, from the way I keep my house, to the behavior I expect from my children, to my unrealistic expectations of what "success" looks like. Anything short of perfection is unacceptable. It is utterly unattainable and yet it woos me back again and again.

The worst part is how it influences my parenting. I want to be a kind and nurturing mother, but far more often I am short-tempered, judgmental, and harsh. I see the damage even as the words leave my mouth, but I can't seem to stop them. It feels like failure again and again and again. And the worst kind of failure: the kind that hurts someone else. I am years into my battle with perfectionism and I still manage to mess it up on a daily basis.

Consider your own life for a moment. Are there areas where you have struggled and failed again and again? Write them here.

Perhaps, like me, you feel a sense of hopelessness, like you'll never beat this sin. No matter how hard you try, it keeps entrapping you. Maybe it even feels beyond your control. It is frustrating, and exhausting. "Why can't I just get this right? What is wrong with me?"

How long was Israel cursed to wander in the desert? What can this tell us about how long the process of sanctification might take in our own lives? Do you find this offers a sense of grace in the midst of your difficulties? Why?

In a broader sense, we can't forget that God's curse was specifically timed to see an entire generation die away and a new generation rise up to take its place. It was forty literal years, but it was a thematic "lifetime."

Read Philippians 2:12-13. What two opposing concepts regarding "work" are we called to hold concurrently? Then, read Hebrews 4:11. Can you see two more opposing words that the author is trying to hold simultaneously? How can we "be diligent" or "strive" in seeking "rest?"

Like the Israelites, we fall prey to the idea of self-sufficiency: that it is only through our own efforts that salvation – and, ultimately, sanctification – can be attained. And yes, there is absolutely a part of our journey that must come from recognizing our own sinfulness and actively working to remedy it. But there is also a miraculous part of our salvation that is at work; just as miraculous as the death on the cross and the rising from the dead. God is at work in us, through the power of the Holy Spirit. This, too, should comfort our wounded and weary hearts: the burden of our sanctification is shared.

If we work in tandem with God on our journey of sanctification, what does it mean to you that the burden is shared with the Holy Spirit?

Is the Holy Spirit convicting you that you have been trying too hard to work out your own salvation? Allow Him to share that burden today.

Lesson 9 – Suzerain Treaties and the Structure of Deuteronomy

Prayer

Please open in prayer and initial here. _____

Reading

Core Track: Deuteronomy 6:4-9, 11:18-25
Extended Track: Deuteronomy 6:1-25, 11:1-32

Response

Consider the text of today's readings and their reflections of one another.

Lesson

Deuteronomy is a unique book in many ways, some of which we have already discussed, such as its expository nature in the midst of a linear history of the Nation of Israel. We also briefly touched on the importance of its structure in Lesson 5 when we looked at some of the most common outlines of this book. Today, we will dig a bit deeper into this idea of structure; that is, how the book was written and why it was written that way. In doing so, we will cover one of the most important ways of understanding Deuteronomy, as a Covenant Treaty – also called a Suzerain or Vassal Treaty – a legally binding form of ancient Middle Eastern diplomacy.

What do you think the word "treaty" means? Write out your definition, then look it up in at least two places and add any additional insights.

If we read Deuteronomy within the context of a treaty between God and Israel, what have been some of the critical obligations established thus far on each side?

Israel Will: *God Will:*

The word "covenant" should be relatively familiar to us given that God has already made two of them with Israel prior to reaching Deuteronomy, but it can also be one of those tricky words that we think we understand but really don't. It is worth noting that it can be used as a direct synonym for "treaty" but also can be as straight-forward and simplistic as a basic "agreement."

Read Genesis 17 and list the critical obligations established for each side as part of the Abrahamic Covenant.

Abraham Will: *God Will:*

Read Exodus 20 and list the critical obligations established for each side as part of the Sinai Covenant.

Israel Will: *God Will:*

(Interestingly, Jewish History records yet another Covenant, though it is not included in our Christian text. Called the Noahide Laws, it is a series of seven laws given to Noah upon the swearing of the Rainbow Covenant after the flood (Genesis 9:8-17). It reads as a very early version of the 10 Commandments.)

So, what makes this covenant outlined in Deuteronomy different than any previous version? Many scholars suggest that the first – the Abrahamic Covenant – was a "personal" covenant, one sworn between two individuals, for all that it included Abraham's descendants. The second – The Covenant at Mount Sinai – is a "marriage" covenant, a theme we can see repeated in the New Testament when the Church is referred to as the "Bride" of Christ. This third one, though, is a covenant in the most legal sense of the word. It is a treaty, a legally binding agreement on the part of two international players.

Structurally, Deuteronomy actually follows the outline of a Suzerain or Vassal Treaty: a treaty written between a powerful king or kingdom and a vassal state. Vassal states aren't something we are familiar with in our modern context, but they were common in ancient times, and even as recently as medieval, feudal culture. It is similar to a mutual defense contract, where the greater or superior power commits to aid and assist the lesser power, usually militarily, while the lesser, or vassal state, commits to the sovereignty of the greater, usually with an economic component (think of it like the lesser paying taxes to the greater). As you consider the history of Israel and some of the obligations made thus far on the part of both Israel and God throughout Deuteronomy, is this sounding familiar?

There are two recognized outlines for this type of treaty that modern scholars rely upon, though neither is above reproach given the scarcity of ancient texts to study. The first suggests a six-part structure:

1. Titles   *4. Oaths*

2. History   *5. Blessings and Cursings*

3. Stipulations (or Obligations)   *6. Concluding Rites*

After listing the titles of those involved on the treaty or the sovereign areas in dispute, a history of the relationship is briefly outlined, followed by the rules for a new relationship. Both sides agree and witnesses are called, human or supernatural, to ratify the treaty. Finally, both the benefits of keeping the treaty and the cost of breaking it are listed, as well as an outline of what ceremonies will be performed to conclude ratification.

The second outline has only five parts, similar to the six-part structure but with a few key changes:

1. Preamble   *4. Blessings and Cursings*

2. History   *5. Succession*

3. Stipulations (or Obligations)

Unlike the six-part structure, the oaths and concluding rites are removed from this format but are replaced by a succession clause; that is, how future generations will be required to uphold and enact the given agreement.

If we see God as the Sovereign Lord, or Suzerain, of this type of treaty and the Nation of Israel as the Vassal, we can see the structure of either the six-part or the five-part format clearly expressed throughout Deuteronomy.

Still, the question remains, why enact a third covenant after the previous two? Why change what already exists? To answer this, we must shift from looking backwards into looking forwards, into the future of Israel within the Promised Land. Ultimately, they will be a nation, their own country, with an internal governmental structure and sovereign lands of their own. They will no longer be just a "people," but also a "place." As such, it makes perfect sense for God to adjust His relationship to them from one between individuals to one between powers.

I know this is a lot to take in, but believe me when I tell you that understanding the underlying historical and cultural elements of your reading can do nothing but improve both your understanding and expand your interest. One of my favorite Bible Study quotes come from Jen Wilkin: "The heart cannot love what the mind does not understand.[11]"

With that in mind, we can't wrap up our lesson today without looking at one more critical component of Deuteronomy: chiastic structure. I promised you in Lesson 5 that we'd come back to it, and the time has now arrived.

Pronounced "kī-ah'-stik," this type of structure is one that reflects back on itself and can be found in both micro- and macro-examples throughout the Bible. It is a repetition of similar ideas but in a reverse sequence, sometimes called Reversed Parallelism.

Beth Moore teaches a fantastic lesson on Chiastic Structure in her Bible Study on Esther[12]. In it, she shows how the eight feasts listed in the book reflect one another in an inverted fashion.

The first feast (Esther 1:2-4) is meant to show the sovereignty of the king and as an opportunity for him to show off all his wealth. The last feast (Esther 9:19) is a celebration of God's sovereignty and His deliverance of the people of Israel from the king's proclamation. The second feast (Esther 1:5-8) follows right on the heels of the first and talks about the valuable dishes and decorations that the king used for his own glory. The seventh feast (Esther 9:17) takes place right before the last feast and the verse before (v. 16) talks about all the plunder the Jews *did not* take. The third feast (Esther 2:18) celebrates Esther's elevation to Queen, though her identity as a Jew is still hidden. The sixth feast (Esther 8:17) celebrates the deliverance of the Jewish people from Haman's law by the revealing of Esther's heritage. Finally, the fourth feast (Esther 5:4) lures Haman into an

[11] Jen Wilkin, Women of the Word: How to Study the Bible with Both Our Hearts and Our Minds (Wheaton, IL: Crossway, 2014), 33
[12] Beth Moore, *Esther: It's Tough Being a Women* (Nashville, TN: LifeWay Press, 2008, 2014)

inflated sense of his own importance while the fifth feast (Esther 7:1-6) is the one where he is revealed to be Esther's (and the Jewish people's) enemy. Esther 6 stands as the keystone, or Central Core, of both the book and the feasts. It is the flipping place: the place where the structure turns back on itself and moves in the other direction.

Though some are more easily seen and understood than others, each of these reflected feasts is meant to show a contrast, or an opposite.

On paper, we might see it written out like this:

A. Feast 1 (Esther 1:2-4) _____

    B. Feast 2 (Esther 1:5-8) _____

        C. Feast 3 (Esther 2:18) _____

            D. Feast 4 (Esther 5:4) _____

              E. Central Core (Esther 6)

            D*. Feast 5 (Esther 7:1-6) _____

        C*. Feast 6 (Esther 8:17) _____

    B*. Feast 7 (Esther 9:16-17) _____

A*. Feast 8 (Esther 9:19) _____

Based on the quick synopsis above, jot down the reversal or the contrast that occurs between each pair of feasts on the lines to the right. (Remember, A goes with A; B goes with B*, etc.)*

Now, we're starting to understand what a Chiastic Structure (or Chiasm (kī'-asm)) looks like. But why is it important? To answer this, we must remember two key points: 1. The vast majority of the Bible for the vast majority of history has been taught in auditory form, that is, it was *heard*, not read, and 2. While we read our Bible in English, it was originally written in Hebrew, Greek, and a smattering of Aramaic.

Knowing that the Bible (and the Jewish Pentateuch) was primarily heard instead of read is critical to understand because it reminds us that Biblical authors, especially Old Testament Biblical authors, would have structured their writing in a way specifically tailored to their hearers. There are any number of literary devices included in the Bible that are meant to help hearers better remember what they are learning about. We see it in the 10 Commandments with the five commands about loving God and five commands about loving people. We see it in Matthew's genealogy of Jesus, which divides his lineage into three sets of fourteen (even though, historically, we may be quite sure that there were more generations than what is listed). We see it in Psalms when songs are written in acrostic form, with each line or verse using the next letter of the Hebrew alphabet. All of these are meant to be used as tools to help hearers remember. Don't memorize ten commandments, memorize two groups of five (this is what we do when we memorize a telephone number). Likewise, three sets of fourteen, each specific to a section of Jewish history, is way easier than forty-two names. Can't remember the next line of the song? Which letter comes next?

That last one presses us into our second point: part of the reason we are so bad at seeing these literary devices, these tools and reminders that are built into the Word, is because they aren't written in our language, either culturally (we are not subsistence tent-dwellers in the ancient Middle East) or, quite literally. Acrostic poems in Hebrew don't translate into English well. Don't believe me? Read Psalm 119, the most famous acrostic in the Bible. By the same token, many of the best literary devices for auditory memory don't translate well into reading interpretation. Likewise, we don't "hear" them, even if we were looking for them, because the language has changed. Finally, we aren't really looking for them, because these are literary devices that were popular thousands of years ago, but not so much today. Think about the difference between your High School classics assignments and a modern pulp fiction novel. They *sound* different, and that's only a change of a few hundred years.

How does knowing that the Bible was written in another time and place, and in another language, challenge how you study it? What changes do you need to make, mentally, to better plant yourself in its garden of wisdom?

With all of that said, let's jump back into Deuteronomy. Taken as a whole, scholars Bill Arnold and Bryan E. Beyer[13] suggest Deuteronomy could be divided into one chiasm in the following manner:

A - THE OUTER FRAME:
A Look Backwards (chapters 1-3)

B - THE INNER FRAME:
The Covenant Summary (chapters 4-11)

C - THE CENTRAL CORE:
Covenant Stipulations (chapters 12-26)

B* - THE INNER FRAME:
The Covenant Ceremony (chapter 27-30)

A* - THE OUTER FRAME:
A Look Forwards (chapter 31-34)

Chiasms abound throughout the Bible. Even the Lord's Prayer can be divided into an inverted parallel! However, for today we're going to look at only a basic version. Remember today's reading? Did you notice that though we read a new chapter, we also reflected back on a previous chapter? And in doing so, did you notice any similarities?

If Deuteronomy 6-11 expands upon the First Commandment, it is bookended by our readings from today. And within those bookends exist our starting place for our own chiasm.

Personal Challenge:

Not every challenge we face will be spiritual, though if you are intentional, I think you'll find that even the most mundane among them will leave spiritual gleanings. Today's challenge is all about taking what you've learned and putting it to work, specifically within the framework of understanding chiastic structure.

I'll get you started with your bookends and even offer a suggestion for the central core of your structure. You fill in the rest in whatever way feels most reflective to you. I'll use shapes so you can fill in as many or as few as you'd like; there is no right or wrong way to create an inverted parallel. Ready? If not, that's okay, just give it your best shot!

---

[13] Bill Arnold and Bryan E. Beyer, *Encountering the Old Testament* (Grand Rapids: Baker Books, 1999), 143

- THE OUTER FRAME:
    The Shema (6:4-9)

- THE CENTRAL CORE:
Possession of the Land (9:1)

* - THE OUTER FRAME:
    Repetition of the Shema (11:18-25)

Wow, look at you go! That was not an easy assignment, but I guarantee that there is truth in Isaiah 55:10-11, "As the rain and snow come down from heaven, and do not return to it without watering the earth and making it bud and flourish, so that it yields seed for the sower and bread for the eater, so is my word that goes out from my mouth: it will not return to me empty, but will accomplish what I desire and achieve the purpose for which I sent it."

How has the Word impacted you through today's lesson and what has it achieved?
If today felt like too difficult or cerebral a lesson, consider how your study of Deuteronomy thus far has impacted your thinking or faith.

Lesson 10 – A Resting Place and An Inheritance

Prayer

Please open in prayer and initial here. _____

Reading

Core Track: Deuteronomy 12:1-12

Extended Track: Deuteronomy 12:1-32

Response

What struck you in today's reading? Take a moment to think about it and write any notes or thoughts here.

Lesson

In our last lesson, we wrapped up our study of Deuteronomy 6-11, which, as you may remember from Lesson 7, scholars Andrew Hill and John Walton suggest correspond to the First Commandment. Today, we see how they correspond Deuteronomy 12 to the Second Commandment.

What is the Second Commandment? Try to remember first, but if you can't, you can peek back at Deuteronomy 5:8-10. How does the Second Commandment relate to or expand upon the First Commandment?

Reread Deuteronomy 12:1-4 and list every command Moses gives concerning how to treat the idols of Canaan. Underline any word of these commands that strikes you as particularly strong or emphatic (for example, "utterly destroy" in v. 2).

Once again, Moses is repeating his warning that if the Nation of Israel allows even the tiniest fragment of idol worship to survive in the Promised Land, it will infect the entire population. And it does.

Read Deuteronomy 12:29-31. What does Moses warn that the Canaanites do in v. 31? Read Judges 11 and summarize. How has the idol worship of Canaan completely infiltrated Israelite culture?

*Read 1 Kings 18:20-24, 36-40 and summarize what happens. Five-and-a-half centuries later, what were the Israelites **still** struggling with?*

These are only two quick examples among far too many to list of the price that disobedience continued to extract for hundreds and hundreds of years upon the people even after they entered into the Promised Land. And this was not God's intent for them. Don't miss this key point: God desired good things for His people, and He was bringing them into the Promised Land for a specific purpose.

Reread Deuteronomy 12:8-9. What two phrases does Moses use to describe the Promised Land?

A resting place and an inheritance. I don't know about you, but I could use some rest in my life, today. I have an elementary schooler and toddler, plus a college student living at home. We have a dog and a cat and four chickens. I work as a writer, a speaker, a Guide Dog Puppy Raiser, a First Responder Trainer, and as the Librarian at my son's school, where I am also on the Board. My days are filled with laundry and dishes and to-do lists. I wake at 6:45am and, if I'm lucky, my head hits the pillow at 10:00pm. We don't own a television and I literally cannot comprehend how we would have time to watch it even if we did. Rest sounds awfully nice.

And who wouldn't want a nice inheritance? I wouldn't turn one down, that's for sure.

So, how is the Nation of Israel to come into the promise of rest and abundance? Through obedience to God. Let's take a moment to tie Deuteronomy 12:9 back to the beginning of the chapter, the things God is calling Israel to do in order to move into His promise. Deuteronomy 12:2-3 is meant to stand as a contrast to Deuteronomy 12:5-6, with v. 4 as the keystone between them.

Remember learning about Chiastic Structure? If v. 4 is the Central Core, write a chiasm here that compares and contrasts how Israel is to treat idols versus how they are to treat God. Remember, feel free to add as many layers as you want.

- Outer Frame (v. 2-3)

- Central Core (v. 4)

* - Outer Frame (v. 5-6)

I hope in your chiasm, you caught the importance of location. If you didn't, briefly review these few verses and take a moment to jot down the difference Moses expresses in your notes above. While it was not uncommon for God-worshippers to build altars of remembrance in places where God had met them or provided mightily on their behalf, Moses draws a stark distinction here that he continues in Deuteronomy 12:13-14.

Moses promises that God will establish for the people a place - a physical location - that they might come to worship Him after they have conquered the Promised Land. Where did this end up being?

Why do you think God wanted to establish for Himself a place, a home, if you will?

Personal Challenge:

God has always desired that His people would be a people after His own heart, a people set apart on His behalf.

Read 1 Peter 2:9. How do you think this New Testament verse relate to our Old Testament lesson today?

Read Hebrews 4:14-16. If we are "a royal priesthood," who is our "high priest?" How, then, are we to approach God because of it and what will we receive from Him?

Read Acts 2:36-38. After proclaiming Jesus as "Lord and Christ," what two things does Peter tell the people to do in response (v.38)?

I love Peter's exhortation to repent and be baptized. In it, I see a long line of Old Testament prophets who saw the disobedience of Israel and called them to repentance and restoration. Before entering the Tabernacle, or later, the Temple, the High Priest would ritually cleanse himself in order to be made clean, sin-free (see Leviticus 16). Otherwise, he would be struck down upon entering God's presence. We, too, receive a ritual cleansing when we decide that we desire to enter into God's promised rest and inheritance. We are baptized.

Some scholars believe that the modern idea of baptism actually grew directly from the ritualistic cleansing practices of Leviticus 16, but certainly it was common by the time John the Baptist baptized Jesus.

Read Matthew 3:13-17. Take a moment to picture Jesus, the Son of God, being baptized by human hands. John the Baptist, himself, recognizes the upside-down, backwards nature of this exchange. Now, in the space below, write one large word: the place where Jesus was baptized.

I hope that your heart just skipped a beat. I hope you got goosebumps as you wrote that one word. I sure did the first time I realized the significance of this moment!

Reread Deuteronomy 12:10. What waters would the Nation of Israel pass through in order to enter into the Promised Land?

The commentator Matthew Henry describes Deuteronomy 12:8 in terms of "irregular worship," the idea that cases of necessity can lead to irregularities in worship, but when these necessities end, regular worship must resume. In a modern sense, we can all experience these irregular necessities: an illness or injury, a special school event or meeting. A worldwide pandemic. Any of these might cause us to miss what we would consider to be our regular schedule of worship: our church or Bible Study attendance, etc. But, they do not constitute a new "normal." Once these irregularly scheduled events cease, our worship should resume.

There were many irregularities in the worship of Israel during their wanderings, but Moses is letting them know this will end as soon as they enter the Promised Land. Regular worship will be reestablished, and, what's more, Moses is expounding on how this regular worship should look.

Likewise, before we come to know Jesus, we are each of us doing "whatever is right in [our] own eyes." (Deuteronomy 12:8) But after we meet Jesus, after we are baptized, these irregularities must cease. We are now, as Peter called us, holy: set apart.

What do you think this thematic location — the Jordan River — means in both instances: for Israel and also for Jesus. End our lesson today by taking a few moments to write down your thoughts about baptism, the Jordan River, and entering into the promises of God.

Lesson 11 – Arbitrary Obedience (Is Not So Arbitrary)

Prayer

Please open in prayer and initial here. _____

Reading

Core Track: Deuteronomy 13:12-14:3

Extended Track: Deuteronomy 13:1-14:21

Response

Take a moment to think about what impacted you from today's reading. Consider our Decalogue Framework and how these chapters relate to the Third Commandment.

Lesson

In many ways, Deuteronomy 13 feels like an on-going continuation of our previous lessons, but rather than belabor our previous points, I want to point us in a slightly different direction with today's lesson. Hang on, because we are going for a ride through history.

What did Moses command of Israel in Deuteronomy 13:15-17? Was anything to be spared? Why?

I think we often read Old Testament laws like this one and kind of shrug our shoulders, asking, "Yeah, so what?" Today, I hope you'll see the answer in stark relief.

Read 1 Samuel 15:1-9. What does God command King Saul to do in v. 3? How does this reflect today's Deuteronomy reading?

What does Saul do instead? Why? (See. v. 8-9)

Ultimately, Saul's act of disobedience – not only against God through His prophet Samuel, but also against God's law as provided by Moses – leads to his rejection as king. But, Saul's disobedience doesn't end with his kingship, or even with his life.

Think back to the generational aspects of some of our previous lessons. God promises abundance for obedience not only to this generation, but to those coming afterwards. Likewise, His threats encompass not only those alive now, but those still to come. These are not empty promises. These blessings and cursings that God enumerated were meant to be real, tangible consequences.

Read Esther 3:1-6. What lineage does Haman come from? Where have you seen that name before?

Though Haman's lineage is specifically called "Agagite," if you are perceptive, you'll see the name of the king Saul was *supposed* to have killed: Agag. Haman was an Amalekite, born of the line of a deposed king who should have been killed without "any pity." (1 Samuel 15:3) Saul's disobedience echoed across the ages until his entire people were threatened with death. And why? For the sake of a few sheep and cattle.

Now, lest we judge Saul and think ourselves his superior, I want to take a moment to ask you to step into his shoes. He has an army of 210,000 troops that have been raised from all over the country. They've fought a number of decisive battles and appear to have completely annihilated the Amalekites. As far as we can tell, they've also followed all the other commands of God to "kill their men, women, children, and even their babies." (1 Samuel 15:3) In point of fact, we are told in v. 8 that "every Amalekite was killed except

King Agag." But an army marches on its stomach, and the range of the Amalekites was likely just to the south of the Promised Land, in what most Bible maps label the Desert of Zin. Not a lot of food to be had in the desert, as the people of Moses' time learned during their forty years' wander. Good luck feeding that big army of yours, Saul.

And what about the age-old practice of looting? After establishing this vast army and decisively conquering their enemies, is Saul going to forbid them the spoils? Traditionally, this might be the only form of payment a soldier might receive for his service; meanwhile, his fields at home go untended, his craft unpracticed, his family possibly facing poverty or starvation in his absence. Saul might be brave enough to lead an army against a foreign foe, but he's not brave enough to court starvation and rebellion in his own ranks. Easier to give in than stand firm, especially since his previous actions show who how little regard he holds for God's law, anyways.

Personal Challenge:

From our history lesson today, I want to challenge you in two ways: a micro and a macro. The first, the micro, asks what this means to you, personally.

As you read God's law (as given by Moses), what things in your life have you continued to allow as an idol?

Remember, an idol is anything in our lives that takes a more important place than God. This could be a thing or a practice, but it could also be a person. It could be someone like your spouse or your children. In fact, Satan would like nothing better than to take your love for your family and twist it into something that causes you to undervalue God. He's a sneaky little bugger like that. And, though I'm in danger of becoming repetitive, I draw on Moses as my inspiration. Perhaps you shrugged the first time I asked you. Perhaps the second time you felt the Holy Spirit stirring within you, but not yet enough to give something up that you are beginning to understand needs to be given up. Even as I write this, I will share with you that I, too, am struggling to be obedient.

God has clearly asked me to remain firm in giving something up. It's not something big or ugly or sinful. It's actually the kind of thing that most people would probably not even notice. But He has asked me to do so, and He has called me to be obedient, and that is really hard, because it's something I enjoy a great deal. But if I am a "holy [person]…chosen…to be a [person] for His own possession," (Deuteronomy 14:2), then I can't do anything other than seek obedience.

If God has called for your obedience in something and you are struggling, as I have struggled, I encourage you to write a brief prayer asking Him to help you overcome the desire or temptation.

My second challenge, the macro, asks what this could mean for future generations. How could this small kernel of disobedience grow into a flourishing, deep-rooted weed? When I pause to consider my own struggle, I notice how much time it steals. And not just from me, but from my family, from my children. I notice that their interruptions frustrate me. I notice my words are impatient, perhaps even harsh, when they are only expressing their small, human needs: a snack, a story, a cuddle; attention, time, love. If I don't get control of this small obsession, now, it will, in turn, create fertile ground for my children to grow in flawed ways. In time, perhaps they, too, will indulge similarly, perpetuating this small sin of disobedience, or one like it, on their children.

Many years ago, my mother shared with me what she most regretted about my young years. "I wish I would have read less." Reading. Her own escape from the pressures of being a full-time working mother. Her own sanctuary. A skill that has been valued and lauded in our family. I, too, am a reader. My son, almost eight, has caught the bug, as well. My husband listens to audiobooks because he doesn't have time to pick up a physical one. My littlest loves bringing stacks of picture books to me. Who would have thought something so valued could be so dangerous? And yet, this was the thing she named: reading. Because it sapped her time and attention, stealing it from me and my brother. Instead of parenting us well, she retreated into her own head, into the escapist world provided by another's imagination. I do the same.

How could your sin or idol you listed above become a generational wounding or source of on-going disobedience?

Should I stop reading? Should I cut it completely from my life, like a city burned to ash? I don't believe that is what God has asked of me. But, He has asked me to give up certain forms of reading: certain genres of escapism, certain modes, like having my kindle on my phone (always available, always tempting me). And this is where it is so hard. Why this but not that? Why *yes* here but *no* there?

If you read the Extended Reading today, you ended with a list of clean and unclean animals. If you only did the Core Reading, take a moment to skim the latter part of today's reading. List a few of the clean versus unclean animals.

Clean   *Unclean*

Many scholars have made arguments for the common-sense approach of understanding clean versus unclean animals (edible versus inedible, healthy versus unhealthy, etc.), and perhaps they have a point, but I would argue that these lists are somewhat arbitrary, and that's okay, too. Sometimes, God's call to obedience is somewhat arbitrary. Of course, He wants us to be obedient because He has higher purposes for our lives than simply our own self-satisfaction, but like any other practice, sometimes obedience is simply in the daily repetition of commitment. "I will do it because You have asked it of me." Because, one day, maybe He will ask something of me that seems crazy (like giving up bacon), and I'm a lot more likely to obey if I'm in the habit of obeying than if I'm not.

Has God ever asked you to do something that feels a little arbitrary? How about a little crazy? What was your first response? How did you ultimately choose to act?

Lesson 12 – Rest, Rejoicing, and Restoration

Prayer

Please open in prayer and initial here. _____

Reading

Core Track: Deuteronomy 14:22-26; 15:1-18; 16:9-17

Extended Track: Deuteronomy 14:22-16:17

Response

Take a moment to jot down anything that particularly impacted you through the reading today.

Lesson

I am a do-er. In Biblical parlance, a Martha. Let's be honest, in America today, most of us are Marthas. Very few of us read the story of Lazarus' sisters and think to ourselves, "Ah, yes, I am Mary." We are steeped in a world of tasks and to-do lists, consumed by our comparative culture, even, dare I say it, slaves to our own salvation. Yep, I went there. We have an overwhelming tendency to "work out your salvation with fear and trembling" while simultaneously forgetting that "it is God who is at work in you, both to will and to work for His good pleasure." (Philippians 2:12-13, NASB)

Read Luke 10:38-42. What do you make of Martha in this passage?

Not only are we a world of Marthas, we are exhausted by it. Depending on your translation, we are busy, distracted, worried, upset, anxious, troubled, and bothered. And underpinning all of this is a niggling sense that Jesus' words to Martha are His words to us, today, "Mary has chosen the good part." (Luke 10:42, NASB) We are exhausted Marthas and we are failing to meet Jesus well.

How do we let go of our Martha-esque tendencies and embrace a more Mary-esque reality? I think to do this we need to delve deep into the Old Testament and reconsider everything we know about the idea of rest.

How do you think Mary's "good part" reflects the idea of resting in the Lord, of Sabbath, and of our reading today?

About six months ago, I realized that I was not resting well. I was busy, productive, and efficient, but I didn't feel fulfilled by these things. There were always more chores the next day, more messes to clean up, more dinners to make, and more appointments to meet. As a stay-at-home-mom, I think it can be even more challenging because you live where you work, so you never feel like you can be "done" and "go home" for the day. (Can I get an amen from anyone who has unloaded the dishwasher at eleven at night or found themselves folding laundry in the wee hours of the morning before the kids wake up?)

I began to explore what resting well might mean, and, in true Martha fashion, I added "take a break" to my daily tasks. For a few minutes each afternoon, I forced myself to stop after completing one task but before starting the next and mindlessly scrolled through social media or read a few pages of my book. That is, until the laundry was done, or the puppy whined because she needed to go out, or the toddler shouted from his bed that his blanket had come off. Then, it was back into the rush and the grind, and for all that I'd taken that break, I didn't feel the least bit rejuvenated or restored.

Ultimately, I realized that not only did I not know how to rest well, I didn't know how to rest at all.

Do either of these statements resonate with you today: not knowing how to rest well or not knowing how to rest at all? How have you grappled with this struggle? How has it left you feeling?

I think that we and Martha share a common challenge. We know we should be "resting," but we have no idea why or how. We know that we are to Sabbath, but we don't really know what that means or what it encompasses. Today I want to challenge you with a big idea: that Sabbath is much more than taking a Sunday "off," whatever that means. It is to fully embrace all that it meant for God to "rest" in Genesis; all that it meant for Israel to "rejoice" in the wilderness after their release from Egypt; and all that it means to "restore" ourselves at the end of a season of trial and difficulty. Furthermore, it is to understand that Jesus called himself the Lord of the Sabbath (Matthew 12:8) and the eschatological meaning of his kingdom coming and the rest, rejoicing, and restoration this should bring to our everyday lives. Phew, that's a lot for one little word. So, let's get to it.

Read Genesis 2:1-3. What do you think God did on the seventh day? What did His rest look like?

It is the Hebrew word for "and He rested" that gives us our modern word, sabbath. *Shabath* means "to cease." To stop. And, in conjunction with the previous idea of the completion of the Creation act, the meaning is nuanced and textured. God didn't stop mid-project; He stopped because it was done, accomplished, ended. And then he blessed it. He took joy in His Creation.

When was the last time you finished a project and stopped to take joy in its accomplishment? Was it a piece of artwork or a creative endeavor? Maybe a house project like painting a room or planting a new flowerbed? How did it make you feel to see it finished? Was your joy fleeting or deep and abiding?

The year after we moved into our house, I replanted the bed in front of our porch with tulips, daffodils, and hyacinths. Every year since, I wait with anticipation for the first green shoots of the Spring, then sit back and watch as each plant unfurls its blossoms in its appointed order. I love to watch my flowers come up first in vibrant green leaves, then pink, purple, white, yellow, and red. They bring me joy, the first hint of Spring arriving and ushering in warmer, sunnier weather.

So, the first rule of Sabbath is that it is a time not just to stop, but to appreciate what we have accomplished. Even clean dishes and stacks of carefully folded laundry can point us back to this idea of Sabbath. If God created the world with a precise sense of order, the setting of our homes in order is a small act of the same. We echo God's will for the world in our small sphere and, if we pause, can take the same restful joy in its accomplishment.

Read Deuteronomy 5:12-15. The commandment to Sabbath is closely linked to a specific event in the history of Israel. What is the event and why do you think God relates it to celebrating the Sabbath?

Boy, I hope you took the time to grapple with this question. If not, I really want to encourage you to go back and wrestle it with some more. Sometimes the hardest questions are the ones that bring us the greatest understanding, if we'll let them. I know the first time I read this passage, I had to pause and really wonder how the Sabbath has anything to do with the escape from Egypt. After chewing on it for a bit, I came to a strange realization: I had such a sense inside my own mind of what the Sabbath meant, a preconceived notion, if you will, that my entire interpretation rested solely on that preconceived notion, not on the reality of the Word I was reading. Perhaps you, too, are facing the same gap. You've heard "sabbath" all your life, or at least for all of your church life, and you are so sure you know what it means that it feels all but impossible to connect the idea of sabbath to the story of Israel's escape from Egypt.

So, with that, let's try again. What does Deuteronomy 5:12-15 actually tell us about the Sabbath?

If you're still struggling, I'll give you a hint: it has to do with *who* did the work, and it is a reflection of that Lord of Sabbath I hinted at before that we'll get to soon.

Hopefully, that hint was enough to get you over the hump and notice that the idea of Sabbath, of not working, is in honor of the salvation work that God did *on behalf of* Israel. They did not rescue themselves from Egypt, either in their initial escape nor in their crossing through the Red Sea. Through no work of their own hands did they accomplish any of it, but only by the work of God's hands. Thus, to cease working on the Sabbath is a celebration in faith of the fact that their salvation came not from their own work but from God's. They are to do no work because the work was already accomplished by God. They can add nothing to it, but, it is worth noting, they can take nothing away from it, either.

With this interpretation in mind, take a few moments to form a hypothesis of what Jesus might have meant when he called himself the Lord of the Sabbath.

The Sabbath was not only to be a weekly honoring of God's providential work; it was to extend to a number of annual celebrations of God's provision, as well. Every year, the people were to remember Passover (the celebration of their exodus from Egypt), the Feast of Weeks (the celebration of the day God gave the Ten Commandments at Mount Sinai and also the first harvest of the year), and the Feast of Booths (the celebration of the last harvest of the year). These were all "Sabbath" in nature, celebrations that called for food, drink, family, and rejoicing for what God had done on their behalf.

As modern Christians, we do not celebrate any of these holidays, but our church calendar has its own sacred days of Sabbath: Christmas and Easter. (Thanksgiving could arguably take the place of the Feast of Booths but is largely secular in nature these days.) Though the names and dates differ, we set aside these days each year to remember in faith the work that God and Jesus did on our behalf. We eat, drink, spend time with family and friends, and, above all, rejoice in the work already done. Even in the midst of walking this current world, broken and fallen as it is, we rejoice, as if in the wilderness, that we have been led from the valley of the shadow of death and are journeying towards the Promised Land of heaven.

It is with this deeper understanding of resting and rejoicing in the Sabbath that we can enter into our final point in this lesson: restoration. You see, the Sabbath concept didn't end with weekly remembrances of God, nor with annual festivals. No, Sabbath extended across years and decades.

Reread Deuteronomy 15:1-18. What other times were to be set aside as reflections of Sabbath and what were the people to do during those times?

Even more importantly, with what kind of attitude were the people to perform these acts of restoration (see v. 7, 9-10, 13-14, and 18).

Even as Israel was to spend the Sabbath rejoicing in their own restoration as God's People after their exit from Egypt, they were to extend the same to one another again and again.

Personal Challenge:
The message of the Sabbath is three-fold: rest, rejoicing, and restoration, with all three flowing like streams from the spring of God's provision and providence.

How could Martha have benefitted from understanding the three-fold message of the Sabbath? How did Mary show her understanding of all three by sitting at Jesus' feet and listening?

When Jesus calls himself the Lord of the Sabbath, he is doing as he claimed he would during the Sermon on the Mount: "Do not think that I come to abolish the Law or the Prophets, I did not come to abolish but to fulfill." (Matthew 5:17, NASB) He is fulfilling the very idea of Sabbath in every possible way.

How does Jesus fulfill each of the three-fold messages of the Old Testament Sabbath?

Jesus is the ultimate fulfillment of rest, rejoicing, and restoration, taking all three into himself with his death on the cross and offering all three back to us as we accept his sacrifice in faith. Furthermore, Sabbath is not complete simply in Jesus' death and resurrection. No, because as we look forward towards Revelation and the kingdom coming, we see Sabbath repeated once more, in an eternal, eschatological sense. When all things are once again made new, when heaven comes down to Earth and Jesus returns to sit on an everlasting throne, we will finally enter into the fullness of the Sabbath promise. Not a weekly, annual, or even bicentury understanding of it; not as a moment in time on a cross when heaven and Earth touched for an instant or an hour, but in an everlasting, eternal way.

How will the threefold nature of the Sabbath be fully encompassed in the end times with the arrival of God's eternal kingdom on Earth?

If Sabbath is at once a remembrance of what God has done, a celebration of what Jesus accomplished on the cross, and a practice of the future coming of an eternal Sabbath, how does this begin to shape our understanding of Sabbath as a daily, weekly, or annual practice in our own lives? This is a big question, but it is one worth taking the time to think about.

What does the Sabbath mean to you, now, and how will you celebrate it or remember it differently based on what you've learned?

Lesson 13 – A Levitical Priesthood

Prayer

Please open in prayer and initial here. _____

Reading

Core Track: Deuteronomy 18:1-8

Extended Track: Deuteronomy 16:18-18:14

Response

What did you notice about today's reading that made you wonder or question?

Lesson

It is in today's lesson that we lose the thread, briefly, of our Decalogue outline. This goes to show that no outline, no matter how solid, is truly perfect, but, I believe, also points us back to the beauty of God's Word to live and breathe in ways outside of our human desire for structure and continuity. We were able to track our Decalogue lessons through the first four commandments relatively easily, but at the fifth, it's a stretch to make it fit.

What is the fifth commandment? If you did the Extended Track, did any of your reading today point you towards a better understanding of this law? If you read the Core Track, briefly skim the rest of today's longer reading to answer.

I'll admit, I have a hard time equating this section to its analogous commandment, but perhaps you had better luck than I. Fortunately, a general outline is just that: general. So, with that, I'm going to take a little detour today and pursue a different line of thought, a "tree" lesson, if you will, before we return to the larger "forest." And yet, it is a "forest" lesson, too, in that it will point us, once again, towards a grand, sweeping theme, one which we will see brought to fruition in our next lesson. Let's lay the foundation.

> *Reread the Core Track reading for today (Deuteronomy 18:1-8). What did a Levite give up to become a priest? How do you think that impacted those who answered this calling?*

Keep in mind that the priesthood was born not only of the Tribe of Levi, but specifically of the descendants of Aaron. As such, there was a significant portion of the Tribe of Levi who were not priests. Instead, they were tasked with the care and upkeep of the tabernacle. Thus, though the tribe of Levi was given no inheritance of land in the Promised Land, they were granted a number of cities to possess (more on these cities in the next lesson), ostensibly for those among their tribe who did not enter the priesthood.

In fact, originally it was not a single tribe, at all, who was set aside as a priestly class.

> *Read Exodus 13:2, 12-13; 22:29; 34:19 and Numbers 3:13. Who was originally to be set aside as a priestly class on behalf of all Israel? Why do you think God wanted this kind of cross-section of the population as His?*

One commentary puts it this way: "The fact that God vested priestly functions in one tribe did not release the rest of the nation from their original obligation."[14] This holds important implications for us today, so let's explore it further.

---

[14] "Priests and Levites," Bible Gateway. Accessed May 10, 2020.
https://www.biblegateway.com/resources/encyclopedia-of-the-bible/Priests-Levites

Read Exodus 32:1-10, 19-35. Paraphrase this story, taking special note of the role of the Levites, including Aaron, who was a Levite.

I hope in paraphrasing the story of the Golden Calf, you noticed a complex duality: Aaron, the first high priest, appointed in Exodus 28, a Levite, created the calf with his own hands and led the people in worshipping it, then lied about it (see v. 24). Meanwhile, his fellow tribe members were the first to answer Moses' call. What are we to make of this dichotomy within the tribe of Levi?

What do you make of this duality: Aaron fashioning the Golden Calf and calling the people to worship it while his own tribesmen kill the very people he called into worship? Especially knowing that Aaron will continue as High Priest for many years to come?

As strange as it may seem, I find this dichotomy somewhat comforting, in the same way I see Peter's denial as comforting, or Paul's early persecution of the Church. These are all stark reminders that not one of us is perfect. Not one of us walks out our faith with unfaltering steps. We all flounder and fall, fail and rise again. Sometimes the consequences are brutal, and we may carry our regret for our poor choices for a lifetime, but if only perfect people were worthy of God's love, what hope would there be for us?

Read Matthew 9:9-13. How could these verses relate to Aaron, to Israel as they worshipped the Golden Calf, or to us in the midst of our sin?

So it is in this moment that the faculty of the priesthood passes from the first-born son of each family to a single tribe, the Levites.

Read Number 3:12, 41, 45. What is the final phrase in v. 41 and 45 and is there a comparable phrase in v. 12? Why do you think God ends each verse with these words?

But wait, the story gets even better, because even as the office of ministering to God and the people passes into the hands of this one tribe, it is, itself, a redemptive story of the like only God can commission and create.

Read Genesis 34. Two of Jacob's sons sought to right a grave wrong against their sister. Which ones and how did they do it?

Read Genesis 49:5-7. Do you read these verses as a blessing upon Levi and Simeon or a cursing? Why? What are the consequences of their violent behavior?

Jacob did not forget this event. Many years pass, and still their father harbors the memory of his sons' violence, perhaps further elaborated by their treatment of their brother Joseph throughout his story (see Genesis 37). As a result, he prophecies over them a curse of dispersement, a diaspora that will be repeated throughout Israel's history as the consequences of sin again and again come home to roost.

Personal Challenge:
It would be easy to leave the tribe of Levi here, cursed by their forefather for their violence, but if we did, we would miss God's redemptive power, not only for them, but for us, as well.

Reread Exodus 32:25-29. How has the curse of Jacob become a blessing to the nation of Israel?

The same violence that led Levi and his brother to ruthlessly slay an entire city (which, though never condemned outright is contextually judged as having been outside of God's will), has raised the sword again, but this time righteous anger brings holy judgement, fully within the will of God.

Have you ever used – or misused – your anger as a weapon? What happened and did it ultimately accomplish your goals?

Perhaps anger has not been your challenge, but you resonate with this story in other ways. Perhaps you have a strong sense of morality – right versus wrong – a sense of justice that demands consequences for unrighteousness, spiritual or concrete, but you have failed to temper it with mercy, compassion, and grace. Perhaps you have judged another for their actions while failing to see the ways in which you fail at the very same things.

We can take these moments of harsh self-evaluation and live into the implied cursing behind them, the shame and guilt that naturally accrue in our failings, or we can choose to see them differently.

We serve a God who is both love and justice, jealous anger and extravagant mercy. We are created in His very image, bearers of these same emotions, but fallen, as well. As such, we are doomed to misuse them, misappropriate their purpose, mistake their meaning. But we must never forget that they are the very stamp of God's spirit upon our hearts, and thus, point us towards a higher calling. We can use them for petty purposes or for paramount ones. Our emotions can be a weapon of slaughter or of sanctification.

Can you think of a time when you have used your anger for God's purpose?

This question may be hard for you to answer; I know it was for me. And perhaps that is as it should be. Perhaps our anger, or any other negative emotion, is just too big for our small souls to accommodate justly and righteously.

Read Matthew 5:21-26. How does Jesus render the idea of anger in a new way? With these verses as our model, how are we to live with one another?

This is not to say that there is never any place for these feelings in our lives, only that we must be oh, so very wary before succumbing to them. Perhaps "never" is too strong a word, but it probably shouldn't be more than "very, very rarely," lest we fall from grace into judgement of our brothers and sisters.

Lesson 14 – Every Story Points to Jesus

Prayer

   Please open in prayer and initial here. _____

Reading

   Core Track: Deuteronomy 18:15-19:21; 21:10-23

   Extended Track: Deuteronomy 18:15-21:23

Response

   What did you take particular notice of during today's reading?

Lesson

   A little over a year ago, we began reading *The Jesus Storybook Bible* with my older son. It is a children's Bible that emphasizes the ways in which God's ultimate plan and Jesus's story are woven throughout the entire "big picture" plot of scripture. It has many of our best-beloved children's stories, but it also omits many of those you might most expect to find and includes some surprises. Though I have studied the Bible for years and I am keenly aware of the need to look for Jesus in every corner of the Word, I was amazed at how a Bible written for my seven-year-old son opened my eyes in new and exciting ways. It also opened the door for some amazing conversations about God, Jesus, redemption, and restoration, which eventually paved the way to his salvation.

   Today, we're going to spend a few minutes looking for Jesus in some surprising places.

   To begin, read Deuteronomy 18:15-19 and John 14:9-11. Jot down any thoughts you have about how these two passages align with one another.

Just as the role of the Priest was to bring the people into the presence of God, the role of the prophet was to bring the presence of God into the people. As we reflect on our previous lesson and expand upon it in this one, this visual representation from Catherine B. Walker[15] might help you:

GOD

Prophet ⇩ ⇧ Priest

MAN

Read Hebrews 4:14-5:10. How is Jesus appointed as our High Priest and in what ways does He fulfill the historical priestly role? (Keep in mind that the most important function of the priesthood was to offer sacrifices for sin.)

Read Matthew 27:50-51. What does this "tearing" symbolize in terms of our earlier visual representation of how God and humans interact?

Honesty, I could probably write an entire study guide about Jesus as our High Priest, so before I go off the rails any farther, I want to remind both myself and you that we are laying a foundation for today's lesson. A foundation made up of our last lesson's understanding of the Levitical Priesthood as the priests of God - intercessors on behalf of the people - and Jesus as the ultimate fulfillment of that priesthood. If we're looking for Jesus in Deuteronomy, it's easy to find him in the priesthood. But let's look for him in one more surprising place.

Reread Deuteronomy 19:1-13. Where do you see Jesus in this passage?

---

[15] Catherine B. Walker, Bible Workbook: Volume 1 Old Testament (Chicago: Moody Publishers, 1952), 61.

Did you find him? Don't worry, I had a hard time with this one, too. Fortunately, we are blessed by the many scholars who have come before us, a few of whom have written down their insights into passages such as these. One of my favorites, David Guzik[16], enumerates how the Cities of Refuge reflect Jesus.

1. "Both Jesus and the cities of refuge are *within easy reach* of the needy person; they were of no use unless someone could get to the place of refuge.

2. Both Jesus and the cities of refuge are *open to all*, not just the Israelite; no one needs to fear that they would be turned away from their place of refuge in their time of need.

3. Both Jesus and the cities of refuge became a place where the one in need would *live*; you didn't come to a city of refuge in time of need just to look around.

4. Both Jesus and the cities of refuge are the *only alternative* for the one in need; without this specific protection, they will be destroyed.

5. Both Jesus and the cities of refuge provide protection *only within their boundaries*; to go outside meant death.

6. With both Jesus and the cities of refuge, full freedom comes with the *death of the High Priest*[17].

7. *A crucial distinction*: The cities of refuge only helped the *innocent*; the *guilty* can come to Jesus and find refuge!"

Do you see Him now? Wow! I especially love the sixth point and find it unspeakably poignant in terms of our own understanding of Jesus' sacrifice on the cross and our earlier consideration of Hebrews 4.

Reread Deuteronomy 21:10-23. Can you find Jesus here, too?

This one is hard, too, so in case you couldn't quite find him, there is a beautiful example of subverted expectations in the idea of a father withholding his blessing from his firstborn son and the idea of God allowing the curse of sin to fall upon His firstborn Son. Furthermore, the final verses of this passage point us to the Cross, but I hope you

---

[16] David Guzik, "Enduring Word Bible Commentary Deuteronomy Chapter 19," Enduring Word, Accessed May 23, 2020, https://enduringword.com/bible-commentary/deuteronomy-19/
[17] See Number 35:22-28 for an alternate version of the Cities of Refuge text, including this point about the death of the High Priest.

also catch this additional example of subverted expectations: that Jesus was not cursed, nor was he guilty, and yet his death on a tree removed the defilement of sin.

As difficult as these passages can be to understand, you are doing it! I am reminded of the movie *Ratatouille* where Chef Gusteau states, "Anyone can cook." *Anyone* can study their Bible! *Anyone* can pursue God's Word with passion and purpose, and finds these hidden gems buried in long, winding, Old Testament legalism! *Anyone* can meet Jesus in places they never expected to find Him. I hope you are beginning to see that.

Personal Challenge:

Deuteronomy 19-22 returns us to our decalogue outline, and it shouldn't be hard to guess which commandment these passages align with. We are told bluntly, "You shall not murder," (Deuteronomy 5:17), yet these three chapters offer myriad exclusions and excuses to do just that. In fact, in reading this section, it is easy to understand why Jesus often repeated, "You have heard it said…but I say to you…" during his ministry.

Why do you think Moses felt it necessary to add additional rules and "laws" to the people's understanding of murder? Read Matthew 5:21-48 (you may remember part of this passage from yesterday's lesson). How did Jesus get back to the heart of the original commandments? What other commandments of rules from Deuteronomy do you see Him addressing?

Sometimes, we feel the need to build extra protections into things so that we don't "accidentally" stray across a line. I think of the times I've told my older son to "be nice to your brother," assuming he understood what that means. Of course, that's not pushing, hitting, kicking, etc. But the more he seeks clarification, the more the rules pile up. "Can I run away from him in the yard? Can I play with my toy and ignore him? Can I sing a song he doesn't like, even if he's screaming at me to stop?" I could make rules all day long to show my son what "being nice to your brother" looks like, but fundamentally, a million rules will not change his heart. Then there are the moments I look out the window and see him pushing his little brother on the swing, or the two of them adventuring through the woods on an epic quest, and I think to myself, "This is what 'nice' looks like." His heart is in the right place, and his actions follow.

Can you think of a time when you felt the need to build extra rules around something you thought God was telling you was right or wrong? What did those rules look like? What do you think they revealed about your heart?

Our human capacity to rationalize is truly exceptional, and I do not mean that as a compliment. Given long enough to think about something, it is pretty much a guarantee that we can turn wrong into right through cognitive gymnastics that would leave any sane person reeling. The legalism of the Pharisees makes sense when we begin to understand the truly sinful nature we carry within us.

Yet, Jesus sets us free. He gets back to the heart of what God was asking, and in such poignant terms that we cannot misunderstand Him if, God willing, we have ears to hear. When asked which was the most important commandment, He replied, "You shall love the Lord your God, with all your heart, and with all your soul, and with all your mind," (Matthew 22:37) a direct quote, if you will believe it, from Deuteronomy (see Deut. 6:5).

So what does it mean to love God? And when we ask that question, are we asking it with the right heart? Am I trying to love God with the same heart as my son as he asks for a thousand rules to help define what "love" looks like, or am I trying to love God with a tender spirit and the best effort I have?

To wrap us up today, I could ask you to write out a list of the ways you could love God better, or a treatise on what seeing Jesus as a City of Refuge means to you, but I think that would miss the point of this lesson. Instead, I want to encourage you to take a few minutes to write a love letter to God.

When I was dating my husband, we wrote many letters back and forth. I would find a heavy envelope in my mailbox, or slipped under my door, and my breath would catch as I slid my thumb under the seal. I could hardly wait to see what he had written and I'd read the words with feverish intensity, then read them again to savor them. I'd tuck the letters and cards away in a special box and thumb through them often, rereading his words of love and affirmation and letting them fill empty places within me.

Then, I discovered the Word, God's love letter to each of us. Imagine if we read our Bibles with the same heart as we read those youthful love letters. Imagine if we pored over each verse and chapter like love poetry from our beloved. (Need an example? Check out Song of Songs!) Imagine if we turned to His love letters again and again, letting them fill up the empty places within us with His affirmation. How would we see reading our Bible differently through this lens?

Now, it's your turn. Use this space to write Jesus a love letter, then consider praying it to Him. He loves you, pray in faith for a spirit to love Him back.

Lesson 15 – Rules, Rules, Rules…

Prayer

    Please open in prayer and initial here. _____

Reading

    Core Track: Deuteronomy 22:13-29, 24:1-4

    Extended Track: Deuteronomy 22:1-24:5

Response

    What jumped out at you during today's reading? How have our previous lessons impacted how you read differently?

Lesson

    I was blessed to attend a wonderful Christian university and sit under some very wise and discerning professors during my time there. As a new Christian, I was further blessed by the opportunity to attend a thrice-weekly chapel service with speakers both local and international, from author Mark Cahill, to a South Seas missionary whose life experience was so varied and intense that she was rejected from an early season of *Survivor* because she had "an unfair advantage" in survivalist techniques.

    My freshman year I also took two Bible classes from our university chaplain, a man who truly understood what it meant to shepherd a diverse group of young adults through an age of self-discovery and maturing faith. Above all, he believed in us. He believed in our capacity to seek God for ourselves, to grow into our faith, whether long-held or newly discovered, and to choose for ourselves what to sample from the buffet of Christian experiences available to us – to find our own "callings," if you will.

    I had friends who attended other Christian universities, and, by and large, their experiences were quite different from mine. If I had to sum it up, I'd say that the main difference was "rules." Rules about how to dress and what to say, rules about what movies were appropriate and which books could or could not be read, rules about how to spend time with those of the opposite sex, both in groups and individually. So. Many. Rules. It was exhausting to hear about; I couldn't imagine how exhausting it was to live.

Then, my sophomore year of college, our Chaplain retired and new one came on board. Unfortunately, he was more of the rules-oriented kind of leader. Worse, though he could occasionally secure a great chapel speaker on the foundation of our school's name, more and more often speakers were boring and out of touch. Chapel, now with required minimum attendance, was less interesting, more onerous, and also required more often. I remember complaining to a friend, "I wouldn't mind going so much if it felt worthwhile, but I get more out of sitting in my dorm and reading my Bible."

I'm sure you have similar story: one where the weight of rules and regulations eventually robbed a passion of its delight. Maybe you are a part of the economic rat race and either keeping up with the Jones' or with your co-worker as they rise through the ranks has left you exhausted and burnt out. A career that you once loved has become empty. But the rules say this is how it goes: work hard, make more money, get that promotion, repeat.

Maybe you are a parent slogging through the trenches of the little years (or the bigger years, because honestly, I'm just not sure whether it gets better, or worse, or just different farther along). That moment when the doctor laid your newborn in your arms for the first time is so far in the rearview mirror that you've lost any sense of it, and all you can see now is another mess, all you can hear is another screaming match, all you can feel is a kind of numb exhaustion. Meanwhile, social media is feeding you an endless supply of perfect parents to compare yourself to. "Don't ever yell," "be present to their emotions," "sink your entire identity into raising these precious gifts for the next eighteen years no matter what it costs you." Rules.

Maybe – dare I say it? – it is your faith that is being weighted down with rules. Rules that tell you how a "good" Christian looks, or acts, or speaks, or prays. Rules that tell you how often you should go to church, how many Bible Studies or Small Groups you should attend, how many Missions Trips you should go on, how many dollars you should give. There have been a recent rash of former faith leaders leaving the Church in recent years, citing that somewhere along the way, they lost God, lost their faith. They were drowned by the rules.

If your Bible utilizes section headings, take a moment to flip through Deuteronomy 22-25. How many times do you see a section heading that refers to "rules" or "laws?" Recalling our previous two lessons, why do you think so many rules or laws have been included throughout these chapters?

Remember in our last lesson I talked about my son and how he wanted to ask a thousand questions about what, exactly, it meant to be "nice" to his brother? Think of these next several chapters as Moses trying to tell Israel what it means to be "nice" to each other. Chapters 22-25 align themselves with the last four commandments of the decalogue and their goal is to expand upon the meaning of these basic rules in a way that helps everyone understand what God really meant by "You shall not commit adultery," or "You shall not steal." (Deuteronomy 5:7-8) As such, as you read them, picture in your mind my son, presenting yet another scenario of how an interaction with his brother could look, and asking, "Does this count as 'nice?'"

Reread Deuteronomy 22:22-29. What does this passage say "counts" as adultery? As you read, do you find it weighted in favor of anyone? Why do you think that is?

"Don't commit adultery" seems like such a simple rule, but, as they say, the "devil is in the details." Is it adultery if I'm not married? Is it adultery if they aren't married? Is it adultery if their spouse knows about it and doesn't do anything to stop it? Is it adultery if we don't have sex? Which then, of course, leads into a million questions about what, exactly, is or isn't sex... Do you see how this plays out, both in ancient times and in our own, modern age?

And make no mistake, the devil is, indeed, in the details. If you think for one moment he isn't the one behind this kind of hair-splitting legalism then you don't know the enemy you are facing.

Read John 8:1-11. Summarize what happens in this passage. How did the Pharisees fail to uphold the Law in their challenge of Jesus (hint: see Deut. 22:22-24)?

Read Deuteronomy 17:6-7. How did Jesus' response hearken back to this?

It is worth noting that the context of Deuteronomy 17:6-7 is abundantly clear that if a witness is willing to testify against a sin committed, they must be so certain that they, themselves, are the first to throw a stone. Words were not enough to condemn a person, action must back it up.

The Pharisees were using the woman and this law to trap Jesus. What did they reveal about their own hearts in doing so?

Personal Challenge:

In my notes for this section I have one sentence underlined, boxed, and circled: "Basic human decency is not so basic." It was true then and it is still true today, but what has also remained unchanged is the futility of legislating a change of heart. Whether it is what clothes to wear, what movies to watch, or what hot-button political topic of the day has talking heads screaming at one another, people don't change just because a new rule is made. At best, they grudgingly comply; at worst, they seek every opportunity to circumvent it.

When the Eighteenth Amendment to the Constitution first passed, the Temperance Movement hailed Prohibition as a new era in America. Within only a few years, though, every town in the country had at least one backyard distillery and every family had either an aunt or a grandma making gin in the bathtub. Speakeasies boomed and not even local police had the heart to shut them down. Questionable players entered the scene, mobsters and gangsters who capitalized on providing illegal but widely accepted alcohol and places to drink it, inciting other forms of violence, as well, and sending the whole thing underground, away from the eyes of prudish marms. The same people who had agitated for prohibition now realized that it didn't stop their loved ones from drinking, it only forced them to do it in secret.

So, too, with sin. Making a rule about it doesn't stop it from happening, it only introduces shame, that secretive need to hide lest one be caught, either by those in charge or by the loved ones who would be impacted by it.

Under my underlined, boxed, and circled statement, I wrote some more notes. They are the basis for a new life mission, full of the heart that I believe Jesus brought to the table both in his Sermon on the Mount, which we've already discussed in previous lessons, and in this instance, facing an adulterous woman. Jesus summed up the entire law when he reiterated that the most important command was to love God and love people. He stripped away a long list of rules and forced his listeners to get clear on the heart of God's Law. He said, in essence, that the letter wasn't good enough anymore, but that it was the spirit that counted. He said that if we really loved him, we'd love others well, and that if we are loving others well, we are also loving him.

As you reflect on our last several lessons, how has your understanding of the Law changed? How have you seen Jesus present in its midst?

Write your own new mission statement for life with this understanding of both the Law and of Jesus' fulfillment of it. Bring everything you've learned over the last three lessons, and throughout this entire study, into a few sentences to a paragraph summing up your new understanding.

Lesson 16 – (Church) Life Together

Prayer

Please open in prayer and initial here. _____

Reading

Core Track: Deuteronomy 26:5-19

Extended Track: Deuteronomy 24:6-26:19

Response

What thoughts or questions does today's text leave you with?

Lesson

In 1623, John Donne penned words that would resonate across the ages. "No man is an island entire of itself; every man is a piece of the continent, part of the main." The opening phrase of this poem reminds us that we are ever a part of a whole, and, lest his credentials fall somewhat short (he was a remnant of the Catholic Church in England under Queen Elizabeth II and only begrudgingly joined the Anglican faith, later becoming Dean of St. Paul's Cathedral), his words echo Paul's in 1 Corinthians 12.

Read 1 Corinthians 12:12-27. Do you see yourself as a part of the "body" of believers? Why or why not?

What does it mean to you to be a part of the Church?

As Americans, we have a particular bent towards individualism. It is rooted deep in our psyche, an almost unnoticed cornerstone that stretches from the first settlers and across the vast tracts of the west. We won the Revolution by eschewing regimented military practices and pitched battles, and we won World Wars I and II by turning that same creative, independent, ingenious talent towards industrialization and mobilization. So woven into the fabric of our being is this sense of intrepid, independent individualism that it is all but taken for granted, a shadow structure of our collective being. The great irony, of course, is that it is a trait we all commonly share alongside 250 years of history built on this foundation.

As American Christians, however, this ideal of the individual can also be a dangerous trait, an insidious weapon of the enemy. When our American individualism overtakes our Christian commonality, we are in grave danger of forgetting where our eternal citizenship actually lies.

In point of fact, there is this intriguing tension that winds throughout Scripture that asks us to grapple with the question of the individual versus the body of the Church. Today, we're going to use Moses' prayer in Deuteronomy 26 to explore that tension a little more closely.

As an act of worship and out of thanksgiving for God's provision of the Promised Land, Deuteronomy 26 reminds the people of Israel that their first fruits should be presented to the Lord, dedicated at the temple, and should be accompanied by prayers to that effect. The prayer, itself, stretching from verse five to verse fifteen, tackles this tension of the individual and the corporate in a tangible and interesting way.

If you are willing to mark your Bible, use two different colors to underline, circle, or highlight all of the expressions of individualism versus communalism throughout this section of text (I, me, and my; versus we, us, and our). If you don't want to mark your Bible, feel free to note them briefly here.

Individual   *Communal*

The High Holidays of the Jewish Calendar also reflect a sense of communalism, requiring sacrifices not for individual sins, but for the sins of the whole. On the other hand, many of the types of offerings outlined in Leviticus are individual in nature, for specific sins or blessings. (See Lev. 1:1-6:7 for a complete listing of traditional sacrificial offerings.) Confusing things still further, many of the offerings discussed throughout Leviticus required both a personal and communal aspect. (See Leviticus 16 for a great example of this; Aaron must first cleanse himself, then offer sacrifice on behalf of the people.)

> *Read Genesis 17:1-12. Take special note of where in the Abrahamic Covenant God is speaking of Abraham (Abram) alone and where He is speaking of Abraham and his descendants. How does this passage bring further texture to our discussion of the individual versus the group?*

Daniel provides yet another example of this interesting tension between the individual and the community. One of many taken captive during the fall of the Southern Kingdom of Judah, Daniel 1:8 gives us a sense of the type of man he was.

> *List the characteristics of Daniel found in Daniel 1:4, 8-9, 17, and 19-20.*

It is clear from these passages that Daniel is a righteous young man, upright before the Lord, and recognized and blessed by Him. Yet, he lives in a world where the community of Israel is so broken that they have not only divided into two separate countries, but each has also now completely fallen to outside enemies.

The first half of Daniel is often recognized as a guidebook for how we are to live in a broken and unbelieving world, but I think it also points us towards the reality that both our communal and our individual worship matter to God. Daniel was not spared captivity, despite his righteousness, because the community in which he lived required the discipline of God. This is a powerful truth even today, especially for those of us committed to the individualism of the American ideal. Though we might wish that our fellow Christians have no effect on our own patterns of worship, especially when we disagree with them, the fact remains that they do.

Does it feel fair that Daniel suffered captivity alongside those who "deserved" God's wrath for their idolatry? Why or why not? How does today's discussion about the woven nature of the individual and the community change your perspective?

On our wedding day, the Pastor who married us pointed out the circular nature of our wedding bands. With no beginning and no end, a circle represents eternity. A circle could also represent the on-going, cyclical nature of our study today. Individual and community, community and individual, personal responsibility and corporate experience, and back again. Round and round. We are meant to live in this communal manner, the "body" of the Church, but also personally accountable to God for our own actions. Where does one end and the other begin, or are they really two sides to an eternal coin we cannot hope to understand in this world?

Taken with our recent lessons, the texture of our understanding becomes more nuanced, still. We are not merely going through the motions of communal living, or of individual accountability, but, as Moses says in Deuteronomy 26:16, "be careful to do them with all your heart and with all your soul." The weave grows tighter, the warp and the weft coming together in new ways and with new understanding.

Read Acts 2:37-47. How did the new Apostolic Church further reflect this Old Testament circling of individual and community? If you're feeling ambitious, you might consider Acts 5:1-11. How do these verses function as a counterpoint or inverse to Daniel's story?

The Bible does not necessarily offer us easy answers or prescriptive equations. It asks us to seek, dig deep, consider, weigh, and synthesize our own conclusions. If this lesson has felt confusing, or even merely theoretical to you; if it hasn't offered concrete answers, I encourage you to rest in that place of tension, as much of the Bible invites us into resting in the tension of our lesson topic today. It's okay to not know all the answers. It's okay to leave your Bible Study wondering if you've fully understood it. It's okay to ponder what you've learned for a day, a week, even months and years. Welcome to a life of Biblical scholarship, dear sister!

Personal Challenge:

Cyprian of Carthage, an early Christian theologian, said of division within the Church, "He can no longer have God for his Father who has not the Church for his mother."

What do you think he meant by this phrase? How could it be applicable to today's lesson?

Historically speaking, Cyprian's words came during a time of great division within the North African Church in the third century, AD. Systemic persecution had caused some Christians to recant their faith under fear of - or actual - torture, while others stood firm and, pride-filled at their "greater" faith, declared themselves the "one true church," barring moderates from participating. It is a story that could be ripped from the headlines of today's highly politicized news sources. His plea for unity also echoes Paul's words.

Read Ephesians 4:1-16 and Philippians 2:1-7. Why is there a need for unity within the Church? Why do you think Paul wrote so prolifically on this topic?

Interestingly, Paul, himself, holds this tension of the one and the many in a unique way throughout his letters. Many of them begin with the words "Grace and peace to you," or something similar, and commentators have noted the dual nature of this blessing. Since Paul did not write to individuals, but to churches, the words may be read to mean something along the lines of "graciousness and peacefulness among you and between you" as well as a specific benediction of grace and peace to each hearer of the letter.

Perhaps, Paul's writings on the topic of unity reflect nothing less than that with which Jesus commissioned the disciples in John 17 in his final prayer before his arrest.

Read John 17:22-24. What did unity within the Church and among believers do for the advancement of the Kingdom of God?

Have you contributed to unity within the Church? Have you offered grace and peace to your fellow believers, even where they have differed from you? If not, take a moment to write a prayer of repentance and a renewed commitment to pursuing unity among believers.

Meditate for a moment on the words of Psalm 133. Write out any parts that particularly strike you today on an index card, a sticky note, or below, and consider them over the next few days.

Lesson 17 – To Be Set Apart

Prayer

Please open in prayer and initial here. _____

Reading

Core Track: Deuteronomy 27:1-10

Extended Track: Deuteronomy 27:1-10

Response

Though the text today is short, what questions does it evoke? Perhaps try drawing a picture of what you read to better visualize it.

Lesson

Phew! After weeks of study, we have wrapped up what is known as Moses' Second Speech, an expansion of the Decalogue – the Ten Commandments. It seems wise, then, to pause here and consider some key points of the last twenty chapters before we move into the third and final speech of Moses.

First and foremost, we must remember that the rebuke of the Lord in Numbers 14:20-38 has now been fulfilled. For their disobedience, Israel was cursed to wander the desert for 40 years, the length of a generation, until all of them but Caleb and Joshua had died off.

If the previous generation has all died, who is left now, at this point in the narrative, to hear Moses' speech? What insight does this give you as to why Moses has spent so long recounting the people's history and all the sundry laws?

The idea of a "generation" is flexible, but a simple way to think of it, especially in the Old Testament, is approximately fifty years. We can assume, then, that the eldest of those who are now left, about to enter the Promised Land, would have been only around ten years old at the time of the deliverance from Egypt. Most of those hearing Moses' words this day would not even have been born at the time that God brought them out of slavery.

How does this impact your understanding of the nature of Deuteronomy? Think about why it was necessary for Moses to reiterate so much about their history and the Law. Consider what stories the current generation might have grown up with versus what experiences of God they've had.

A key point to remember in Deuteronomy is that the generation of the Mount Sinai Covenant is dead. Moses is, in essence, starting over. In fact, if you read the Sinai Covenant chapters alongside some of these Deuteronomy chapters, they are remarkably repetitive. This is on purpose. God, through Moses, is renewing His covenant with *a whole new people.*

Another key point of Deuteronomy is in regards to the laws, themselves. In short, commentators remind us that we should not be reading Deuteronomy through modern eyes as a list of rules to be followed. Instead, we should be asking two questions. First, for what purpose they were given.

Why do you think God gave the Ten Commandments and allowed Moses to expand the people's understanding of them in these last twenty chapters?

Leviticus 11:45 suggests a possible reason, and one I find compelling. "For I am the Lord who brought you up from the land of Egypt to be your God; thus you shall be holy, for I am holy." (Lev. 11:45, NASB)

What does it mean to "be holy?" This word in Hebrew, *qadowsh*, means "sacred" or "set apart." In essence, they were to be "set apart" from the world because God, Himself, was "set apart" from the world. These laws, then, were not given to be a list of arbitrary rules, but in order to set the people apart from those around them. Set them apart, how? By calling them to a different way - a higher way - of living than their neighbors.

This brings us to the second point in regards to the Law. If the purpose was to help "set apart" the people who practiced it, we must ask, set apart from what? The answer, of course, is set apart from their peers, the other cultures and civilizations of the Ancient Middle Eastern world. Thus, many commentators believe that we should not be concerned quite so much with what each individual law says, per se, but in how each one differentiates Jewish culture from the prevalent cultures around them.

For example, it was common among virtually every other culture of that age to have a pantheon of gods and goddesses. The very first commandment, however, instructs, "You shall have no other gods before Me." (Deut. 5:7, NASB)

In Lesson 7, we studied this passage. Recall an alternative translation for the word "before." If you can't remember, flip back and check. How does the very first commandment set Israel apart from its neighbors?

Consider the other nine commandments. If each of them aligns to a way that Israel is set apart from other nations, what can we assume, even without intense historical study, about some of the cultures surrounding them?

A final point to consider - because I don't want you to come away with the idea that the Law is nothing but an ancient, relativistic exercise with no bearing on our modern life - is how each individual law reflects the heart of God, and it is in this final exercise that we can begin to see Deuteronomy not only as an ancient set of practices, but also as a modern model. Perhaps we are not called specifically to be careful of whether what we are eating is clean or unclean (see Acts 10 and Romans 14 for more on this), but might it be worth our time to consider whether what we are "consuming" is clean or unclean (think in terms of technology, culture, social media, etc.)? Perhaps we are not building stone altars to idols in our modern age, but might it be wise to ask whether we are building spiritual altars in our hearts to such things as fame or finances?

Personal Challenge:

Each lesson in this study has begun by inviting you to respond, however briefly, to that day's text. Often, when something intrigues or challenges us, it is an opportunity to go deeper and learn more. It is both the Holy Spirit's way of prodding us in a given direction and the beautiful way in which God's Word can meet us in our minds as well as our hearts. And I bet, given the nature of Deuteronomy, if you've participated in this activity, you've probably made note of a law or two that has left you scratching your head.

I heard a sermon once on Deuteronomy 25:4, a single verse, but one that Paul specifically references in 1 Corinthians 9:9. Alone, I never would have considered it of any account. It doesn't even make sense! But within the larger context of Paul's words, suddenly it takes on new life.

> *Read Deuteronomy 25:4 and 1 Corinthians 9:3-14. How does Paul's explanation in Corinthians teach us what this single, tiny law in Deuteronomy means? What is the "heart" of God behind it?*

Now, it's your turn. Flip back through your responses, or even flip through the pages of your Bible over the last twenty chapters. Find that niggling question, that law that makes no sense, or that you didn't even understand when you first read it. Turn it over. Munch on it. Pray over it and ask the Holy Spirit to reveal new wisdom and insight. Plug the verse into Google with the word "commentary" alongside it and see what others have had to say. It might take some digging. You might not actually find an answer. Be okay with that and continue to chew over it for a few more days. Get curious. Get excited! You're in the trenches of true Biblical scholarship, now, sister! Way to go!

> *What verse did you choose to study? What did it end up meaning? Did you find God's heart behind it? If not, did you learn something different? Use this space to journal your exploration, how it made you feel, and what you learned.*

Lesson 18 – Blessings and Cursings

Prayer

Please open in prayer and initial here. _____

Reading

Core Track: Deuteronomy 27:11-14, 28:1-37

Extended Track: Deuteronomy 27:11-28:68

Response

What did today's text leave you wondering about or questioning? What stood out to you? How did it make you feel?

Lesson

I am so excited to get into today's lesson because there is just so much here for us to chew over, especially as we trace some thematic threads through our reading. Let's get right to it!

Read Genesis 49, the deathbed blessings of Jacob over his many sons, and make note of which sons receive blessing and which sons receive cursing. Do any sons receive a more neutral-feeling word? Now, note which tribes were to stand on the mountain of the blessing and which were to stand on the mountain of the cursing in Deuteronomy 27:12-13. Do you notice anything about how Jacob's prophecies relate to the later tribal locations? I've done the first one for you.

Son/Tribe Name	Blessed/Cursed/Neutral	Mountain
Reuben	Cursed – "you shall not have preeminence"	Ebal/Curse
Simeon		
Levi		
Judah		
Zebulun		
Issachar		
Dan		
Gad		
Asher		
Naphtali		
Joseph		
Benjamin		

It is worth noting that any time you come across the name of a tribe or the name of a location, especially in the Old Testament, it probably has some thematic relevance beyond just a name. It is always wise to take a moment to check back and refamiliarize yourself with its significance. Conversely, you can use a Concordance to look ahead, as well, and see if any future references might link back to your passage. We will do this again with the Tribes in just a few chapters, but for now, let's jump ahead to the next book in our Bible.

Read Joshua 8:30-35, a common Concordance cross-reference for both "Gerizim" and "Ebal." What does this passage describe? How does it relate to today's Deuteronomy passage?

This location, the valley between the mountain of Gerizim and Ebal, has even further significance. Turn to the map on page 123 of this workbook and find Mt. Ebal and Mt. Gerizim. Find the Salt Sea (Dead Sea) and slide your finger north until you reach Succoth, then west towards Shechem. Draw a large circle around both mountains. Then, take a moment to remind yourself of Israel's current location during Deuteronomy, just east of the Jordan River, on the Northeast end of the Salt Sea (Dead Sea), near Mt. Nebo. Keep in mind, too, that the conquest of Canaan, the Promised Land, has not yet begun, and in just a few chapters, Joshua will commence this conquest by marching across the

Jordan and taking Jericho, the first city to fall. Looking at this map, think about how far Israel must go to reach these mountains of blessing and cursing. How many cities will they need to take? How many months of war will they face before standing in the valley between Gerizim and Ebal?

Note the geographical location of these two mountains within the region: dead center. Many commentators note that in order for Moses' commands in Deuteronomy 27 to be fulfilled, the conquest of Canaan will have to be all but complete, given that these two mountains are deep in the heart of the territory Israel is to take.

Finally, note the important city which sits in the valley between these two mountains: Shechem. Thematically, this city is critical for two reasons. First, it is the most centrally-located City of Refuge set apart in the new land (recall from Lesson 14 the significance of the Cities of Refuge). Secondly, it plays as important a role in the death of Joshua as we will soon see our current location plays in the death of Moses. In fact, if you read the last chapter of Deuteronomy (especially within the context of understanding its place within the entire book of Deuteronomy) and the last chapter of Joshua, they are remarkably reflective of one another!

Read Joshua 24 and discuss all the ways it recalls our entire study of Deuteronomy thus far.

Personal Challenge:

The Cursings and Blessings of Gerizim and Ebal hinge on a critical – if tiny – word: *if.* As Joshua will challenge the people on his own death bed, Moses is making clear that he is setting before the people a choice: obedience or disobedience, and the attendant consequences thereof. But, as we have discussed in previous lessons, it is not simply purposeless obedience or disobedience. The choice, and the consequences, have a much greater purpose than illustrating the vagaries of an autocratic god.

Why was Israel being called to obedience? What larger purpose was their obedience to serve? (For a reminder, flip back to Lesson 17 and remember the meaning of "holiness.")

Guzik has been and remains one of my favorite commentators, and we will turn to him again, here, as we consider the consequences of this set-aparted-ness and God's greater purpose within it.

"God was determined to reveal Himself to the world through Israel. He would do this either by making them so blessed that the world would know only God could have blessed them so; or by making them so cursed that only God could have cursed them and cause them to still survive."[18]

The enumeration of the blessings and cursings illustrate this point: blessed beyond all human understanding or cursed beyond all human understanding, either way they would testify of the Living God to the nations.

And testify they did. If today's lesson leaves you wanting more, I encourage you to dive deep here, and explore the fulfillment of the blessings and cursings that Moses presented:

- Deuteronomy 28:9-11 versus 1 Kings 10:1-13
- Deuteronomy 28:32-33 versus Daniel 1 and 2 Kings 24
- Deuteronomy 34 versus the "Sign Acts" of Ezekiel 4-5
- Deuteronomy 28:36 versus, again, Daniel 1 and the Babylonian Diaspora, as well as the Roman Occupation of Jesus' time
- Deuteronomy 28:49-52 versus the Roman Occupation of Jesus' time and the massive famine that followed the destruction of the Temple in 70AD
- Deuteronomy 28:53-57 versus 2 Kings 6
- Deuteronomy 28:68 versus 68AD and following when there was such a glut of Jewish slaves in Egypt that they were literally un-sellable

However, should you need a possible breath of hope, I'd suggest you glance ahead a chapter to Deuteronomy 29:4 and compare it with Ezekiel 36:26 and the indwelling (and outpouring) of the Holy Spirit in Acts 2. There are some powerful things happening in these passages not only in terms of fulfillment of prophecy, but also in linking Old Testament prophecy to New Testament prophecy, and the greater (or better) fulfillment that Jesus brings as the promised Messiah.

As we settle for a moment, then, here in the New Testament, I want to take a moment to point out one final thought.

---

[18] David Guzik, "Enduring Word Bible Commentary Deuteronomy Chapter 28," Enduring Word, Accessed September 12, 2020, https://enduringword.com/bible-commentary/deuteronomy-28/

Read John 14:12-15 and 23. Note our tiny hinge word – if. Does this "if" imply a different kind of covenant promise between the hearer and Jesus than the blessings and cursings we've been studying? Why or why not? Are these "if's" linked to blessings, cursings, neither, or both?

There is a danger in reading the Old Testament, written specifically to and for the Jewish people, through modern, Gentile eyes. It would be all too easy, I think, for us to draw the conclusion that, like the ancient Israelites, we will be so blessed or so cursed by God for our obedience or disobedience that we, too, become the testimony to the nations. Like Job's friends who saw his cursing as the result of his unnamed or unacknowledged sin, we can easily fall prey to a kind of prosperity gospel that sends the insidious message that because we are blessed, we must be acting in obedience, or, conversely, because we feel cursed, we must be acting disobediently. Perhaps there is a place, corporately, as the Church Body, to understand it in this way, but we cannot read and understand these frameworks without acknowledging the ways that Jesus' coming turned them all upside-down.

From the idea of "dying with Christ" or being "crucified with him" to the assurances of both James (1:12, 5:10-11) and Peter (1:6, 2:20-24, 4:12-14) that we will, indeed, absolutely, without question suffer for our partnership with Him, Jesus' life and ministry negated the idea that the obedient Christian's life would reflect nothing but blessing. Before that, David lamented throughout the Psalms that even good people face unfair treatment, even unto death, and the greatest hope we have in the face of such evil is to cling to faith that God sees us, even in our suffering.

The belief that obedience = automatic blessing and disobedience = automatic cursing is far too simplistic a view for us to take. Even if it was a general rule in Old Testament theology, we still see the example of Job to remind us that no rule exists without exceptions. The New Testament goes farther, turning our understanding of blessing on its head through the example and calling of Jesus.

Arguably, no one in the New Testament was more obedient or faithful than Paul, yet he suffered constantly for the gospel. Peter, as well. Page through Acts and jot down as many instances of suffering these men faced as you can find: beatings, imprisonments, shipwrecks, etc.

What message ought we to take away from these examples?

How do we synthesize an understanding of the Blessings and Cursings of Deuteronomy 28 with the example of Jesus, Peter, and Paul as to the suffering of obedient believers? Are they completely incongruent or can you find some common ground?

These are really hard questions, ones that theologians today still grapple with and find nigh unanswerable. Do not kick yourself if you, too, struggle to come to some workable conclusion. As I said at the end of the last lesson, you are, indeed, in the trenches of true Biblical scholarship, a lifelong journey, filled with unanswerable questions this side of heaven. But oh, like any truly great adventure, it is not the end result, the arrival, that holds the most value, it is the journey. Take the scenic route, get off the highway, wind through a valley or up the side of a mountain, pause and marvel at the view. There are blessings here to be had.

Lesson 19 – Commissioning

Prayer

    Please open in prayer and initial here. _____

Reading

    Core Track: Deuteronomy 31:14-29

    Extended Track: Deuteronomy 29:1-31:29

Response

    How did today's reading land with you? Did it further expand upon the themes of our previous lesson? In what ways?

Lesson

    As we barrel towards the end of Deuteronomy, I can't help feeling like there is so much richness and depth we haven't had time to explore. There is a beautiful chiastic structure in chapter 30 that I could write a whole lesson on, there are textures of blessing and cursing still to be explored, there is still more prophecy embedded in the text that we haven't considered and seen brought to fulfillment in later books. Deuteronomy is not a book that one reads only once, then moves on, and I hope these remaining questions, these themes and thoughts, will draw you back, again, to this book, long after our study is done.

    Nevertheless, as we come to the final speech of Moses, we can see many of the major themes we've explored thus far brought full circle and to fruition. The commandments have given way to the consequences: blessing or cursing, and Moses, himself, knows that death draws near.

Reread Number 20:2-13 to remind yourself why Moses was not permitted to enter the Promised Land. How do you think he felt at this moment? How have you felt immediately after sinning and realizing the consequences of your sin? By the end of Deuteronomy, is there any indication of how Moses feels, knowing that this is his final speech to Israel?

As Jesus did during the Upper Room Discourse, Moses knows that his time is drawing to a close, and the previous few chapters illustrate this fact. His final exhortations to the people are more and more impassioned. *Obey*, he advises them. *Remember*, he begs them. *And when you don't, you will suffer*, he warns them, repeatedly.

Nevertheless, his work is all but done, and for all their disobedience and rebelliousness, Moses loves his people. He cannot leave them leaderless on the cusp of the Promised Land.

Based on your memory, where does Joshua, Son of Nun, first show up in the Bible? What story comes immediately to mind as an introduction.

Chances are, you went straight to the story of Joshua, Caleb, and the other spies entering the Promised Land, then returning in fear. Only Joshua and Caleb had faith that the Israelites could overcome the "giants" in the land. It's important to note, however, that Joshua's first appearance on the scene predates this one.

Read Exodus 17:8-16. What role did Joshua play in this text? Did he do well?

There are two key points that we are to take away from this first appearance of Joshua. The first is that his role was clearly defined and carefully delineated as different from that of either Moses or his brother Aaron. Though he would succeed Moses as leader of Israel, he would not succeed him as the *spiritual leader* of the people. He would succeed Moses as the *military leader* of the people.

The second key point is more subtle. Since we know that the battle with Amalek occurred before the spies entered the land, and since we know that it was only after the spies entered the land that Israel's lack of faith was rebuked and punished with forty years of wandering, it is arguable that Joshua has spent the last forty years under the tutelage of Moses. In fact, Joshua and Caleb are the only logical choices to succeed Moses: the only two who were clearly experienced enough commanders to join the spy mission and clearly faithful enough to trust that God would provide the victory. We aren't told why Joshua was chosen over Caleb, but Number 27:15-23 shows that it was not only Moses' will that Joshua succeed him, but, far more importantly, it was God's will.

God is about to force a transition in leadership. It will be a forced transition because, by His will, Moses will not enter the Promised Land, but, even more so, it will be forced because Moses is about to die. After forty years of leadership, after being the voice of God to the people for an entire generation, he is about to leave them. And he *must* leave them.

What do you think the danger might have been in allowing Moses to continue to lead the people after they entered the land (assuming his disobedience at Meribah was a non-issue).

Moses is an archetype of Jesus. He was the savior of Israel, leading them out of Egypt by the hand and will of God. I use the term *archetype* to provide clarity that he was, obviously, not Jesus, but his entire life, and his position in the life of Israel, was meant to point towards God's greater plan of salvation from sin. However, the danger with any archetype is that it is mistaken for the real thing. After forty years of hearing God through Moses, a generation removed from the slavery of Egypt, it would be so easy to conflate Moses with the coming Messiah. Even to conflate Moses with God. In fact, such a danger was this that we will see in our final reading that God didn't even give Israel the body of Moses. He wasn't willing to risk that kind of idolatry. Even more important, though, by preventing Moses from entering the Promised Land, God was forcing an even greater transition than the military leadership.

What other transition of leadership do you think God was forcing? Hint: think about what type of leader Joshua was to be and what type he was not to be.

Not only was a military transition occurring, a spiritual transition was occurring. Aaron has already died, the Levitical Priesthood has been established, and now, Moses, too, is leaving them. Joshua will not step into the role of spiritual leader, and though the office of High Priest will remain; theoretically, if practiced correctly, the people will not make the mistake of seeing the High Priest as God. (In fact, we see the truth of this in 1 Kings as Elijah clearly occupies the position as High Priest and the voice of God but not being mistaken for God, Himself.)

So, who would now be the Spiritual Leader of Israel?

Personal Challenge:

It was not only Ancient Israel who was in need of a Spiritual Leader. We, too, face this dilemma, and while earthly leaders can point us in the right direction, as even the best of the High Priests did for Israel, so, too, can earthly leaders fall prey to sin. For every Elijah there is an Urijah, who replaced the altar of God with an Assyrian altar (see 2 Kings 16:10-16). For every Aaron, there are his two sons, both burned by fire for their disobedience in their worship (see Leviticus 10). Eli, himself, was both a great judge of Israel and a father who loved his sons too greatly to properly rebuke them (see 1 Samuel 2:22-25 and 3:11-14). For every great pastor or preacher, even today, there is another who has been carried away by his sin, sometimes within the same person.

Who then, do we look to?

In Lesson 10, we discussed Jesus as our High Priest in some depth, and I hope that His was the first name that came to your mind. Of course, we can rely on Jesus for our Spiritual Leadership. But I want to invite you to expand that list, as well.

Read Deuteronomy 30:6 and Ezekiel 36:25-28. What does God promise in these passages? How does this relate to the idea of spiritual leadership?

In Lesson 5 we dug in a bit in understanding the indwelling of the Holy Spirit, but I want to point us to one more place that will further illuminate the role of the Holy Spirit in our spiritual leadership.

Read Romans 15:14-21. What is the work of the Holy Spirit in this passage?

In fact, many commentators divide the work of the Trinity into 1. God the Father, who plans, 2. Jesus the Son, who executes, and 3. the Holy Spirit, who sanctifies.

What does sanctify or sanctification mean to you now? How has your understanding or definition changed since we last studied it?

Sanctify or sanctification comes from two Latin words: *sanctus*, which means holy, and *fiacre*, which means to make. Thus, literally, it means "to make holy." It is the work of the Holy Spirit in us that makes us more and more holy, helping us identify our sins, confess and repent, and grow in our capacity to do better.

Thus, the search for a Spiritual Leader in any age begins and ends with the One who is the only one worthy of such a role. So it was to be as Ancient Israel entered the Promised Land, reliant upon God for their spiritual needs. So it ought to be for us, today.

Moses was a good leader, but he was not perfect. His own imperfections meant that to idolize him was to fall so, so short of God's plan. They were called to more. Likewise, we are called to live under the headship of a High Priest who is also one with God. To accept anything less is to live under a weight that falls far too short of God's ultimate plan for our lives.

This does *not* mean that we shouldn't sit under the authority of wise and discerning teachers, compassionate Pastors, or reverent Reverends. Nor does it mean that we should quit the fellowship of believers and Sunday Church. Scripture clearly calls us to these things. But we must keep these people, these human, sometimes sinful people, in their proper place within the hierarchy of our faith. And that requires that we know intimately what our faith entails. How are we to test the truth of any teacher's words if we don't first know the truth for ourselves?

Have you fallen prey to idolizing a Pastor, teacher, or even a political figure and made the mistake of putting them above the spiritual headship of the Trinity? Idolatry abounds in our lives even today, and Satan loves to hide it beneath our Christian practices. Ask God for help identifying these sneaky forms and confess and repent, if needed. Reaffirm His headship over your life, by Jesus Christ and through the sanctifying work of the Spirit.

Lesson 20 – Hope

Prayer

Please open in prayer and initial here. _____

Reading

Core Track: Deuteronomy 32:1-43; 34:1-12

Extended Track: Deuteronomy 31:30-Joshua 1:9

Response

What are your final thoughts as Deuteronomy wraps up? How do these chapters sum up the book or pave the way for the future? What questions linger from the text?

Lesson

You have made it, dear sister! 20 lessons, 34 chapters, 10 commandments, 1 covenant. Wow! Take a moment to celebrate all that you have learned. Praise God for His mercies, which have opened your eyes to the wonders of His word. Praise Jesus for the work which He accomplished to fulfill the promises of the Covenant. Praise the Spirit for His small voice, guiding and directing your study over this past season. Holy is the Lord, and worthy of praise!

I love that as Deuteronomy comes to a close, we find Moses, too, praising the Lord. When He has accomplished something great, our first instinct should be to worship.

What has God accomplished that Moses should sing a song of praise to Him? What purpose does Moses' Psalm in Deuteronomy 32:1-43 serve?

In our last lesson, we picked up the drumbeat of Moses final speech: remember, obey, or suffer the consequences. This final song of Moses is his last opportunity to impress upon the people this critical call to faithful covenant life. Yet, as we have seen time and again, the call is tempered by his knowledge that they will forget. They will disobey. And they will suffer.

As we close Deuteronomy, though, I don't want to leave us in the hopeless place of faithlessness, brokenness, and sin. Yes, Israel will fall short (as we do). Time and again we will see them overcome by sin, perverting the ways of God, turning to false idols, being overcome by pride and greed, and we could easily see Deuteronomy as nothing more than the opening scene of a great morality play that will continue throughout the Old Testament, a prescriptive of what not to do.

But if we did that, we would miss the beautifully redemptive work of a God who does not abandon His people. Not then, and not now. If Moses' chief theme over his three speeches is to *remember*, we cannot miss the chance to see this theme play out across the next two thousand years.

Read 1 Samuel 10:25. What is Samuel doing as he prepares the people for their new king?

Read 2 Kings 22:8-23:3 and 2 Chronicles 34:14-21. What lost book do you think was found in the temple? What actions did its discovery precipitate?

Read Nehemiah 8:1-12. What does Ezra read? How do the people respond?

Read Romans 7:4-12. How do Paul's words echo the response of Josiah upon rediscovering the book?

Again and again, we see that the Law, though it condemns sin, also convicts the heart. As grace-filled, Jesus-loving, New Testament Christians, it is all too easy for us to look upon the Law of the Old Testament as little more than an archaic morality code. A list of rules to follow that are both arbitrary and impossible. Outdated, overturned, a symptom of a culture we cannot hope to fully grasp or comprehend. Dear one, I hope after this study you no longer see the Law this way. Perhaps we are exempted from it by our faith in Jesus, but it is not worthless. Through it, we see the character of God revealed, His love for His people, His faithfulness to them, and above all, a harbinger of Jesus and the Spirit coming.

Read John 16:5-11. What reasons does Jesus give for the Holy Spirit's coming?

After the indwelling of the Holy Spirit at Pentecost, Peter preaches to the people. Read Acts 2:37-41. Though Peter's words "pierced" their "hearts," who do you think was already at work, even before the promise of the gift in v. 38?

Oh, sister, my heart leaps at the beauty of this Book, written across thousands of years by the hands of dozens of men, for our edification. My spirit trembles at the conviction it brings, but also at the hope that never falls short. Surely, we will be challenged, stretched, even humbled by its words, but we will never be left in darkness. We are sealed by the Holy Spirit, a promise and a pledge, proof of our inheritance (Ephesians 1:13-14). We are justified by faith, through grace, once for all. That is never in question, even in the darkest times. Though we might quail, fail, fall short, stumble, even fall, we will never be abandoned. Do not confuse the process of sanctification (our work alongside the Holy Spirit) with the sealed promise of justification (God's work through Jesus) already accomplished on our behalf.

Personal Challenge:

I cannot close the pages on Deuteronomy without one last beautiful reminder of the hope of God. As these verses end, we find Moses upon the mountain, looking out over the fullness of the Promise. It is not yet accomplished. It is not yet even begun. There are battles still to come, years of war to wage, kings to rise and fall, exiles and diasporas and ingatherings as the people of God work out the Law, for better or for worse. But Moses will not be a part of it. His place in the story is coming to a quiet, secret close.

He will not enter the land. He is forever barred by his own sin.

And yet...

Read Matthew 17:1-8. Who do Peter, James, and John see upon the mountain with Jesus?

Dear one, my eyes just filled with tears. My chest constricted. My breath caught. Do you see it? *Behold!* Moses is there, in the Promised Land.

And was there ever any doubt? Because the Promised Land is not just Israel, not just tracts of land bequeathed to a people of God's own choosing. The Promised Land is so much more.

As a New Testament Christian, what does the idea of the Promised Land mean to you?

I want to make sure we are not confused as we close out our study. The Promised Land is rooted in a location for a reason. Israel was to exist at a crossroads of the spiritual and the physical, twin thematics that would call them to live among the nations, but set apart from them, as well. Likewise, we must live the same way, rooted in the present, crossing the Jordan, baptizing and battling. We are anchored in this world for a reason. Matthew 28:19-20 tells us why. Yet, we exist in another world, too, living in the hope of the kingdom coming, acting out that kingdom in our daily walk. It is a high calling. It is a lifetime endeavor. It is a heroic mission.

Let's get to it.

Map of Ancient Israel

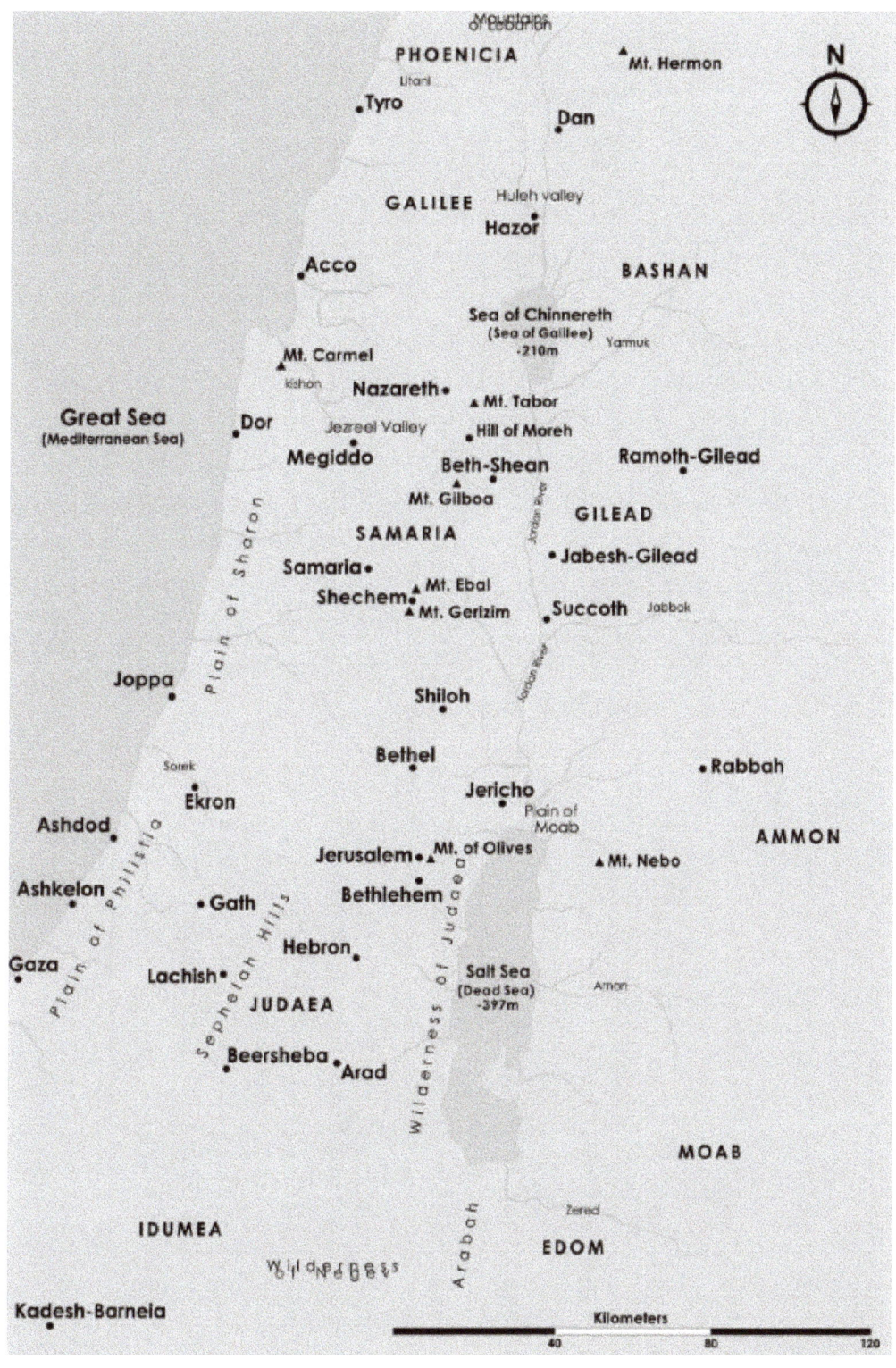

Acknowledgments

First and foremost, I'm grateful to the faithfulness of our God who has called me to this ministry and equipped me to execute it by His good grace. He has never left me nor forsaken me, even in the darkest times, and He will never leave or forsake you, either.

Writing, though a solitary endeavor, is never done without an innumerable cast of behind-the-scenes support. Whether it was babysitting during writing sessions; gifts of coffee, notebooks, and pens; the invitation to speak and teach; or faithful prayer on my behalf, I am indebted to Barb, Jan, and Ulli. They were also my incredible beta readers and caught all my mistakes, large and small. Shannon, for hours of Couch Theology and unwavering love across all that life has thrown at us since I passed you a proverbial note in Bible Study asking if you'd be my friend. You checked "yes" and we've never looked back.

Finally, Eric. Love of my life, father of my children, my biggest cheerleader for twenty years, now. I love our adventure together!

About the Author

     Rebecca Minelga is an author and speaker who uses the power of words to navigate the liminal spaces between who we are and who we are becoming. She raises Guide Dog Puppies and two sons - in that order - with her husband just north of Seattle. She has been previously published in *The Mark Literary Review*, *Crêpe and Penn*, *The Hooghly Review*, *Roi Fainéant*, and *Wild Ink*, and her debut novel, *Third and Long*, is due out Summer 2025 with Conquest Publishing. When not writing, she can be found Open Water Swimming in her local lake, exploring the National Parks with her family, or traveling the world on An Adventure!

Find out all about her latest projects online at www.rebeccaminelga.com.

Printed in the USA
CPSIA information can be obtained
at www.ICGtesting.com
LVHW060933040624
782221LV00017B/203